Decorating for Christmas

At Historic Houses

Decorating for Christmas

At Historic Houses

Patricia Hart McMillan & Katharine Kaye McMillan, Ph.D.

Schiffer Publishing Ltd
4880 Lower Valley Road • Atglen, PA • 19310

Other Schiffer Books By The Authors:

Christmas at Historic Houses. P. H. McMIllan & K. K. McMillan. ISBN:978-0-7643-3559-4. $45.00
Designing and Living with Glass Tiles: Inspiration for Home and Garden. P. H. McMillan, L. H. McMillan, & K. K. McMillan. ISBN:978-0-7643-3206-1. $24.95
Glass Tile Inspirations for Kitchens and Baths. P. H. McMIllan & K. K. McMillan. ISBN: 978-0-7643-2500-4. $19.95
Contemporary Villas: Dialogues with Nature. David Strahan, K. K. McMIllan, & P. H. McMIllan. ISBN: 978-0-7643-3774-1. $59.99

Library of Congress Control Number: 2011928754

Designed by Danielle D. Farmer
Cover Design by Bruce Waters
Type set in Edwardian Script/Souvenir/Arial

ISBN: 978-0-7643-3839-7
Printed in China

Schiffer Books are available at special discounts for bulk purchases for sales promotions or premiums. Special editions, including personalized covers, corporate imprints, and excerpts can be created in large quantities for special needs. For more information contact the publisher:

Published by Schiffer Publishing Ltd.
4880 Lower Valley Road
Atglen, PA 19310
Phone: (610) 593-1777
Fax: (610) 593-2002
E-mail: Info@schifferbooks.com

For the largest selection of fine reference books on this and related subjects, please visit our website at **www.schifferbooks.com**
We are always looking for people to write books on new and related subjects. If you have an idea for a book please contact us at the above address.

This book may be purchased from the publisher.
Include $5.00 for shipping.
Please try your bookstore first.
You may write for a free catalog.

In Europe, Schiffer books are distributed by
Bushwood Books
6 Marksbury Ave.
Kew Gardens
Surrey TW9 4JF England
Phone: 44 (0) 20 8392 8585
Fax: 44 (0) 20 8392 9876
E-mail: info@bushwoodbooks.co.uk
Website: www.bushwoodbooks.co.uk

Dedication

For unto you is born this day in the city of David a Savior, which is Christ the lord.

—Luke 2:10, KJV

Merry Christmas

Very special thanks to our editor, Nancy Schiffer, and her dedicated staff, whose excellent efforts make *Christmas At Historic Houses* and this companion, *Decorating for Christmas at Historic Houses*, must-read books. We gratefully acknowledge the contributions of all who devote their time and talents to keeping historic houses alive and a vital part of evolving history. These houses and their personnel are heartily acknowledged:

Adams House Mary A. Kopco, Kate Bentham, Rose Speirs
Bidwell Martha L. Dailey
Baldwin-Reynolds Joshua F. Sherretts
Bartow-Pell Mansion Amanda Kraemer
Billings Farm Susan Plump
Biltmore Kathleen Mosher, Andy Pearce, Erica Daves
Bingham-Waggoner Estate Janeen Aggen
Blithewold Eileen Miller
Butterworth Center & Deere-Wiman House Angela Hunt, Calvin B. Taylor, Edward H. Hammond, Jr., Susan Taylor
Campbell House (St. Louis) Andy Hahn
Campbell House (Spokane) Joyce M. Cameron, Patti Larkin, Marsha Rooney, Jill Strom
Chief Vann House Julia Autra
Chinqua Penn Plantation Lisa Yamaoka Phelps, Yanida Campa at Renegade Holdings, Laura Pearce, Lynn Umstead Crocker, Kim Parr, Marcia Swiderski
Colonial Williamsburg Jim Bradley, Kathy Dunn, Marianne Martin, Kathy Rose, Meredith Sprinkle, Kathy Wallace, Karam Hwang
David Davis Mansion Marcia D. Young, PhD
Drayton Hall Natalie Titcomb
Flagler Museum John Blades, Amanda Wilson
Florence Griswold House, Tammi Flynn, Rebecca Giantonio at Pita Communications
Gallier Hermann-Grima and Gallier, Stephen A. Moses, Lisa B. Samuels
Hazelwood Wendy Barszcz, Chris Dunbar
Hearth Northington Plantation George H. Northington IV, Janet Hobizel
Hearthside Homestead Kathryn A. Hartley
Hearthstone Christine A. Cross
Joel Lane, Kathleen C. Ruse
John Lind House Trudy Beranek, The Red Hat Ladies
LBJ Ranch The late First Lady, Lady Bird Johnson; Lynda Bird Johnson Robb Shirley James; Barbara Biffle; Judy Callen; Elizabeth Hansen; Margaret Harman, Sherry Justus, Virginia Kilby and Simone Poulaine, U.S. State Department, Rtd.
Leu Robert Bowden, Mantana Brown
Marjorie Kinnan Rawlings Kathleen E. Carr
Marshal's House & Jail Janeen Aggen
Maymont Carla Murray, Dale Wheary
Molly Brown House Annie Robb
Monticello Kim Curtis, Sharon McElroy, Wayne Mogielnicki
Morris-Butler House Shannon Borbely, Gwendolyn Raly
Mount Clare Museum House Michael Connolly, Jane D. Woltereck, and Kathleen G. Kotarba, Baltimore City Department of Planning
Mount Vernon Dawn Bonner, Patty Balladares, Mary V. Thompson
My Old Kentucky Home Alice Heaton, Jean Unglaub
Oldfields-Lilly House Katherine B. Zarich
Petersen Amy A. Douglass
Pettingill-Morron Amy Kelly
Physick Estate Jean Barraclough
Pittock Mansion Lucy Smith McLean
Richards-DAR Sallie M. Grow
Riversdale Ann Wass
Samuel Cupples Petruta Lipank, Mary Marshall, Bridget Fletcher, Neil Metzger
Sherwood Davidson Emily Larson
Slifer Gary W. Parks
Tudor Heather A. Bartlow
Vaile Mansion Janeen Aggen
Van Cortlandt Manor Rob Schweitzer
Villa Finale Rob Abodeely, Michael Anderson, Sylvia Hohenshelt, Margaret Nowack, Sandra Smith
Waddesdon Vicky Darby
Wade David M. Simmons
Webb-Deane-Stevens Charles T. Lyle

Contents

Style For All Seasons

1

Historic Houses Inform and Inspire

Historic Houses are striking examples of personal style. Architects, interior designers, and artists find them sources of endless inspiration. Decorated to dazzle, they are especially exciting at Christmas, a good time to take notes and take home wonderful design and decorating ideas.

ARCHITECTURAL STYLES of historic houses vary greatly in America. They range from the pre-Colonial Van Cortlandt Manor house in upstate New York, to early and late Colonial-era homes like Bassett Hall in Colonial Williamsburg, to the elegant Italianate Villa Finale in San Antonio, to French Chateaux-style mansions like Oldfields-Lilly, to the 1930s Cracker-style Florida farmhouse of Pulitzer prize-winning author Marjorie Kinnan Rawlings. Owners of these houses chose a particular style that suited their personal taste, time, circumstances, and ambitions.

In more instances than not, the term "architectural integrity" to mean "purity of style" doesn't apply. Historically, architects and homeowners combined elements from styles and Periods to suit their fancy. Georgian farmhouses are retro-fitted with Federal entries or Dutch dormers, the smoking room in a French chateau-style house gets a Moorish ceiling, and so on. It's easy to assume that when it comes to architecture, all are free to follow this lead, using taste as the guiding design principal. As for taste, that is hard to define. One wag explained that there was no such thing as good or bad taste; one either had taste or not. It's always a subject for endless debate, cut short by the statement, "I know what I like" (and will pay for). That explains the architectural variety on any given block on any street in America, where one is free to express personal preference. Of course, what one likes one year is apt to change the next. Jefferson changed Monticello, and Washington transformed Mount Vernon, setting the example for future home owners.

INTERIOR DESIGN AND DECORATION may or may not follow architectural style. Bassett Hall is consistently classical Colonial style,

1 Bassett Hall's classic 18th century Colonial style is perennially America's favorite. *Photograph by Barbara T. Lombardi, courtesy Colonial Williamsburg Foundation*

2 Red and Green is the official Christmas color palette for all styles and Periods, but at Oldfields-Lilly, blue is a favorite. *Photograph courtesy Indianapolis Museum of Art (IMA), Oldfields-Lilly House & Gardens*

3 Scandinavian folk art style reigns at the Petersen House in Tempe, Arizona where paper-clip ornaments decorate the tree. *Photographs courtesy Tempe Historical Museum/ Petersen House Museum*

4

5

beginning with the exterior and throughout the gracious interior. Timeless, the influence of this style is broad and a perennial favorite all across the United States. Tweaking the classics by architects, interior designers, furnishings designers, and creative homeowners is an endless game that keeps this adaptable style evergreen.

With some architects, builders, interior designers and homeowners, the mix is what matters. During the Victorian period, it was not uncommon for owners to ignore an essentially Italianate style exterior with its emphasis on elegant verticality, and decorate the interior with ornately embellished curvilinear rococo furniture. Villa Finale very successfully does this, combining furniture and accessories of many styles and periods in an exuberant eclecticism.

COLOR AND COLOR SCHEMES in historic houses may be unexpected. Not all historic houses are drab! There are bound to be colors to please every personal palette. On-going research continues to uncover original colors that surprise and delight. At Monticello, dining room walls boast a newly-discovered original wake-up yellow-gold color. Truly a "good cheer" color, it is thrilling to know that this is the color that Jefferson chose for this room where he entertained so frequently. Rose-pink walls at the elegant Bassett Hall and Buttersworth Center/Deere Wiman houses are

4-6 Bright colors, bold pattern, luxurious textures and too-much-is-never-enough design philosophy were hallmarks of the exuberant Victorian style that has never been entirely out of style. *Photographs by Bobbi Meldahl, Ryan Meldahl, and Emily Larson, courtesy The Sherwood-Davidson House*

6

*At Christmas, Victorian style culminates in a crescendo of **"hey, look at me"** decorations that cover every inch of every conceivable surface in controlled chaos.*

lovely and lively. Rose-red seen on walls at the Morris Butler House in Indiana and the Leu living room in Florida covers walls across the country. Joyful bright red walls at the Vaile Mansion in Independence, Missouri are never out of fashion. To use red, one needs only the courage of conviction. Light colored walls at Mount Clare seem both contemporary and timeless.

7 Decorating naturally—using evergreens, twigs, branches, dried plants, seedpods, and flowers from the garden—is an old practice that grows ever more popular. *Photographs courtesy Calvin B. Taylor House Museum*

8 Gold ornaments in a crystal bowl are a classically simple centerpiece for the holiday dining table at Bassett Hall. *Photograph by Barbara T. Lombardi, courtesy Colonial Williamsburg Foundation*

8

9 Early Christmas trees were tabletop trees, like this one at Bassett Hall, the Colonial Williamsburg home of preservationists John D. Rockefeller, Jr. and Abby Aldrich Rockefeller. *Photograph by Barbara T. Lombardi, courtesy Colonial Williamsburg Foundation*

10 Family mementos as ornaments give a Christmas tree personal style. *Photographs courtesy Calvin B. Taylor House Museum*

Color accents on doors (like the deep green doors at the Calvin Taylor and Sherwood Davidson houses), fireplace mantels, inside corner hutches and cabinets (like that in the kitchen at Pettingill-Morron) are timeless design ploys to enliven interiors.

ACCESSORIZING—the finishing touch that brings rooms to life—is non-stop in historic houses. Decorating naturally—using materials found in yards and gardens—is an old custom once again *au courant* among eco-conscious decorators. Marjorie Kinnan Rawlings decorated her living room and dining room mantels with local vegetation and homegrown fruits. At Billings Farm, evergreens from the farm forest grace holiday mantels and form swags for the staircase. At Van Cortlandt Manor, native plants form a traditional Kissing Ball, forerunner of mistletoe. While materials are natural, personal style may be rustic or refined, casual or formal, artlessly simple or artfully sophisticated.

CRAFTING CHRISTMAS DECORATIONS is a good old idea that has never gone out of style. Scandinavian cut-paper decorations like those at the Petersen House are intricate, requiring instruction. These might be executed in papers that determine the style: handmade, matte finish or coated stock, foils or other. Of course, the idea is simple enough for easy adaptation. For example, children might cut out coloring-book images, add ribbons, and hang them on a tree.

DECORATING WITH FRUIT is an idea seen in every house. Simply stacking fresh fruit in bowls is easy and effective. Mixing fruits with greenery, ribbons, and ornaments is an easy-to-emulate idea that can look dramatic. Studding oranges, grapefruit, and lemons with cloves in interesting patterns and stacking them in bowls to use as centerpieces is an old-and-good idea. Besides looking pretty, citrus fruits add a scent that is synonymous with Christmas.

Earliest historic houses may have been restrained in their use of accessories, even during the Christmas holiday season. But, the Victorian love of ornamentation reached its zenith in Christmas décor. This was the time to pull out all the decorating stops. At Christmas, Victorian style culminates in a crescendo of "hey, look at me" decorations that cover every inch of every conceivable surface in controlled chaos. In this energetic style, to paraphrase beloved Architect Morris Lapidus, too much is never enough! It appeals to those fearless collectors who share his sentiment, so "de-clutter" is not a word apt to be heard in Villa Finale.

Historic Houses of all Periods and styles—rustic or refined—seem to agree that Christmas is the ideal time for decorating. In America, each one is free to pursue life, liberty, happiness, and a personal decorating style.

Villa Finale

2

San Antonio, Texas

Villa Finale is the creation of Walter Nold Mathis, a dedicated preservationist and passionate collector of fascinating artifacts. True, the house has a long history, but to visit the 1870s Italianate limestone dwelling at 401 King William Street is to walk into his world—his vision realized. Villa Finale is both a unique personal decorating statement by a gifted intuitive interior designer and a private museum. When Mathis died at age 86 in 2005, he left his home of 35 years and his incredible collections to the National Trust for Historic Preservation. After a meticulous million-dollar refurbishing, doors to Villa Finale opened to the public in October 2010. During Christmas 2010, the public for the first time could see the house as Mathis would have decorated for the holiday season. Curator Margaret (Meg) Nowack describes Christmases past:

In 2007, while cleaning objects in Villa Finale, I occasionally found remnants of Christmas greenery in the bottoms of vases and vase-like vessels—evidence of use. This was pretty exciting, because a lot of collectors don't actually use their things. I enjoyed knowing that Mr. Mathis had live greenery and flowers around at holiday time.

I can only imagine the grand display that Mr. Mathis had. I never saw it first-hand, but I know that he purchased dozens of red poinsettia plants. He would pile them in the kitchen to give away to family, friends, and party guests. Hanging in the kitchen was a wreath made of hunting gear, including bullets and the prey. For holiday parties, there was always plenty of food set up in the kitchen (and on the dining room sideboards).

Naturally, in proper Walter Mathis form, sideboards and other surfaces would have decorations in bowls and urns, along with live greens and flowers set atop ribbon-festooned tables.

One of the most amazing Christmas-related things I catalogued was a group of Meissen figures that Mr. Mathis had artfully arranged in faux greenery. Each little figure was attached to the greenery so that all one had to do was take it out of its box and put it on a table.

The pièce de résistance of holiday décor was his Christmas tree. His own creation, the tree was comprised of a metal frame in which he would stick Noble Fir branches to create a very long, lean tree suitable for his center hall with its 14-foot high ceiling. In later years, when assembling the large tree became too much trouble, Mr. Mathis placed tabletop trees throughout the house.

Villa Finale is a delightful mixture of elegant Styles and Periods, beginning with the intriguing Italianate street-front façade and inviting Victorian rear porch. *All photographs by Barbara Justice*

The House

Villa Finale, generally described as Italianate, is an interesting mix of architectural influences (original and added over time) including Spanish, English, French Empire, Italian, and Victorian. The overall effect is elegant, romantic, and gracious.

The history of 401 King William Street begins in 1869, when three lots (1.5 acres) were purchased by hardware merchant Russell C. Norton and his wife, Ellen. In 1876, their one-story, four-room house by builder/architect Francis Crider (designer of San Antonio's Travis Park United Methodist Church in 1886) was constructed on the site. Between 1876 and 1879, a second floor was added.

Over the years, this remarkable house endured much change. Due to a financial downturn for the Nortons, in 1882 cattleman Edwin Polk bought it. Over the next year, he added a rear wing and outbuildings. In 1895, the Polks lost the house to foreclosure. From 1908-1917, Eva and Dwight Potter owned the house, calling it Norwood.

The San Antonio River, key to the city's existence, flooded the downtown in 1921, putting it under 12 feet of water and causing widespread devastating damage, including the King William area. Over the coming years, the area which had once been home to the elite of San Antonio declined. In the 1940s, the housing shortage encouraged dividing grand old house into apartments. The house at 401 King William became known as the Women's Building, housing WWII military wives. This area and the house continued to decline over the coming years as the automobile made access to new northern suburbs easy. In the 1960s, highway planners decided a new, more efficient north/south highway was needed and designed Route 281.

To make way for the new highway which was to go through his Mulberry Street yard, Mathis sold the property and went house-hunting. He saw the eight-unit apartment house at 401 King William Street and bought it from owner James Campbell in 1967. In consultation with Architect O'Neil Ford, Mathis (an investment banker) put 16 men to work for two years to restore the house as a single-family dwelling. The limestone exterior was cleaned and the roof repaired. Stained-glass windows were replaced, new copper plumbing pipes installed and historic hardware returned. Inside, partitioning for the eight apartments was removed and the interior refurbished. A gazebo and formal garden were added. Mathis named his new and—by his own design—last home, Villa Finale.

After he had finished restoring Villa Finale in 1969, Mathis set about restoring 14 other houses in the King William neighborhood, including the Chabot House at 403 Madison. Restoration of these properties—some fully restored by Mathis, others financed by him making restoration by others possible—revitalized the King William area and helped ensure his investment in a house that he loved.

Opposite: The entry hall is first of astonishing spaces in the house that Walter Mathis rescued, restored, and furnished as a private museum filled with a dazzling array of remarkable collections of art and artifacts.

Indeed, despite the staggering number of items, there is a mood of surprising serenity that invites lingering.

In 1971, Villa Finale was placed on the National Register of Historic Places. In 2003, Walter Mathis received the DuPont-Crowninshield Award, the highest honor bestowed on an individual by the National Trust for Historic Preservation.

In 2004, Mathis donated Villa Finale and his collections to the National Trust. Following his death in 2005, the National Trust assumed ownership. In consultation with Fisher-Heck Architects, Mainstreet Architects, and Con-Cor Construction a $1million dollar restoration began. The newly-refurbished house was opened as a museum house to the public in October 2010.

The center hall floor plan is orderly and traffic flows easily from the long and spacious hall to all areas of the house. On the right of the elegant entry door is a double parlor. Here is the lavish Napoleonic collection—said to be the most complete in the nation. On the left is the library housing the splendid book collection, followed by the formal dining room, butler's pantry *cum* bar, and kitchen. In the kitchen is a custom cabinet

1

designed by Mathis that incorporates a wall-hung cabinet salvaged from another old house. Here high "plate rail" shelving is filled with his delightful collection of platters. At the end of the long entry hall, a stairway leads to second floor bedrooms and a charming sitting room that overlooks King William Street. From this room—furnished with Victorian seating upholstered in red silk—a circular stair leads to the tower, a distinguishing characteristic of the popular Victorian-era Italianate architectural style. All rooms throughout Villa Finale are furnished with interesting furniture and intriguing objet d'art, arranged with great care. Each is uniquely captivating.

The Collections

The architecture is arresting, but the collections are riveting. Both the breadth and depth of the collections is astounding. Nowack recalls the process of cataloging and photographing each of the 12,500 items. She lists them: American and English china, apothecary jars, coins, paperweights, German beer steins, Mexican War memorabilia, Napoleonic items, 19th century carnival figurines, pewter plates Russian icons, shaving mugs, silver, snuff boxes, stick pins, Texas furniture, Texans campaign ceramics, and time pieces (in one room, the ticking of clocks is noticeably audible). There are Texas landscape paintings and cowboy portraits, including work by noted Texas artists Mary Bonner, and Julian and Robert Onderdonk. And, in the library are the books.

1-2 The entry hall is first of astonishing spaces in the house that Walter Mathis rescued, restored, and furnished as a private museum filled with a dazzling array of remarkable collections of art and artifacts.

3 Displays of groups of items cover every surface throughout the house, including this desktop.

4

5

6

The Mathis Style

The interior of Villa Finale is a visual feast. All surfaces—walls and tabletops—are covered with extensive groups of items—signature of the Mathis style. Most of the 12,500 objects are openly displayed, as though Mathis might return any moment to pick up a small sculpture or rearrange the entire group, as he often did. Sandra Smith, Director of the new museum says: "Virtually everything (with the exception of a few pieces moved out of concern for visitor or object safety) is precisely where Mathis placed it. He had arranged everything so harmoniously that even though there are a lot of items the effect is not overwhelming." Indeed, despite the staggering number of items, there is a mood of surprising serenity that invites lingering. It is not possible to rush through these rooms.

No right-minded person would utter the word "de-clutter" in the filled-to-the-brim rooms of Villa Finale. "He had a good eye and arranged his collections in such a way that items relate to one another," says Smith. "For example, the collection of platters and pitchers installed on shelves high above kitchen cabinets are grouped by country of origin." While most collections are on tabletops or open shelves, others are contained. "Mathis built wooden display cases for his vast collection of shaving mugs; He artfully arranged snuff and pill boxes in small vitrines," says Smith.

4-6 The dining room mantel, sideboard, and table are decorated in-season and out with items that command attention, like the collection of ceramic figures that dominate the table.

No right-minded person would utter the word "de-clutter" in the filled-to-the-brim rooms of Villa Finale. "He had a good eye and arranged his collections in such a way that items relate to one another,"

Mathis' aesthetic sense ruled even utilitarian areas. Nowack points out that in the kitchen he stashed away less attractive spices, but pretty spices were (and are) on stylish display in clear bottles. This simple, effective decorating idea and the many others throughout his glorious home are a gift in perpetuity from Walter Mathis to all who visit Villa Finale.

7-8 Mathis lined the walls of his library with carefully-catalogued books, then accented the area with paintings and objects of interest. It is said that this was his favorite room.

9

Villa Finale's Walter Nold Mathis 1919–2005

- *Walter Nold Mathis descended from the first Spanish settlers who came to San Antonio from the Canary Islands in 1731.*
- *Mathis's family, traced back nine generations, included John W. Smith, the last messenger to leave the Alamo during its occupation by the Texians. Smith later fought at the Battle of San Jacinto, and was mayor of San Antonio under the Republic of Texas. There were two mayors in his family, and many civic leaders.*
- *A southeast Texas town, Mathis, is named for his ancestors*
- *Mathis, a WWII veteran, was an Army Air Corps pilot whose squadron was involved in the Normandy invasion. One of 28 survivors, he was awarded three Distinguished Flying Crosses and a Presidential Citation.*
- *A University of Texas graduate in business, he became a stock broker and investment banker.*
- *Mathis is known as the pioneer of the restoration of San Antonio's Historic King William District.*

9-10 Bright blue enlivens kitcher walls, creating a lively foil for the myriad wall-hangings, shelves of collections of china, and items that interested Mathis. An extensive collection of platters are arranged by country of origin.

11-12 The second-floor hallway is furnished as though it were a sitting room, replete with handsome scrolled-arm sofa and an upright piano. Walls are covered in art from Mathis's extensive collection and everywhere the eye wanders are art-filled vignettes.

13

14

15

16

17

13-14 At one end of the spacious hall, two rooms are treated as a double parlor. Elegant seating includes a chaise lounge and numerous side chairs. In the front parlor, a circular stair leads to the tower.

15 Tabletops are not bare at Villa Finale, but are feasts for the eye and intellect.

16 A Christmas-themed quilt covers a guest bed. It is on the bed "sidewise," just as Walter Mathis always placed it.

17 The Villa Finale Christmas tree ornament is available in the Gift Shop at the Villa Finale Visitor Center.

Bassett Hall

3

Colonial Williamsburg, Virginia

Bassett Hall's 18th century style inspired houses across America. It seems at once familiar, and like an old and dear friend, welcoming in season and out. Yet, this simple frame house is central to the most remarkable preservation effort in the United States.

In 1936, John D. Rockefeller Jr. and his wife, Abby Aldrich Rockefeller purchased the house, which is located on the south side of Francis Street near the Capitol. During the late 1930s and '40s, they restored it and Abby Rockefeller furnished it with folk art. Bassett Hall—which sets on 585 acres, surrounded by lawn, garden, and woodlands—was their home during twice-annual visits during the early days of their astounding restoration of Williamsburg's Colonial area, now known as the Historic Area.

1-2 Bassett Hall is classically beautiful in all seasons. This simple frame house was home to John D. Jr. and Abby Aldrich Rockefeller during their stays while underwriting and overseeing the restoration and preservation of Colonial Williamsburg. *Photograph of house in snow by Barbara T. Lombardi; house in Spring by Judy Marx; courtesy the Colonial Williamsburg Foundation*

It seems at once familiar, and like an old and dear friend, welcoming in season and out.

2

3

4

5

3-4 Holiday accents and a plaque featuring white pine, magnolia leaves, holly, foliage, osage oranges, apples, and red berries decorate one door, while the other is swagged with magnolia, apples, acuba, chinaberries, osage oranges, and pine cones. *Photographs by Judy Marx, courtesy the Colonial Williamsburg Foundation*

Rockefeller was impressed by the history of Bassett Hall. Philip Johnson, a member of the House of Burgesses from King and Queen County, Virginia, built the house between 1753 and 1766. Around 1800, it was purchased by Burwell Bassett, Martha Washington's nephew, for whom it is named. Prompted by the Rev. Dr. W.A.R. Goodwin of Bruton Parish Church in Williamsburg, who passionately believed in preserving the Colonial area, Rockefeller devoted himself to that enormous project. Abby was actively involved and it was she who persuaded her husband to buy Bassett Hall.

After the Rockefellers purchased the house, it remained in the family until 1979. Then, it was bequeathed to Colonial Williamsburg. The Rockefeller's granddaughter and her husband, Abby and George O'Neill, provided the money to restore Bassett Hall and its gardens. Following an extensive two-year renovation of the property, the home was reopened to the public in December 2002.

Much has been written about John D. Rockefeller Jr. and his wife, Abby Aldrich Rockefeller. When they married, he was the son of the richest man in America; she the daughter

6

5-6 In the morning room, the ornamented Christmas tree sets before the window. *Photograph by Barbara T. Lombardi, courtesy the Colonial Williamsburg Foundation*

7 Christmas decorations highlight the mantel in the Bassett Hall parlor which, like the entire house, was thoughtfully decorated for both comfort and charm. *Photograph by Barbara T. Lombardi, courtesy the Colonial Williamsburg Foundation*

8 A feathery tabletop Christmas tree on a small pedestal table lights up a dining room window. *Photograph by Barbara T. Lombardi*

9-10 On the long dining table, a crystal bowl filled with shining ornaments is flanked by candlesticks with tall white tapers and crystal swan bowls filled with ornaments. *Photograph by Barbara T. Lombardi, courtesy the Colonial Williamsburg Foundation*

of the most powerful member of the U.S. Senate. He was shy, she was not, yet both valued privacy. Both, it is reported, considered money's real value to be a tool for good. They devoted their lives, considerable talents, gifts, skills, and money to achieving extraordinary good for generations who will never know them, nor be able to thank them personally. Yet, because of their vision and generosity, all may walk through a thoroughly restored Colonial Williamsburg and Bassett Hall, home of the exemplary Rockefellers.

Christmas In Colonial Williamsburg

The first Sunday in December opens the Yuletide Season in the authentically restored village of Colonial Williamsburg. Musical performances take place on several stages. Visitors, who may stay in the Williamsburg Inn, stroll along streets decorated in the famous "Williamsburg Look." The enchanted evening ends with a bang—fireworks known as the Grand Illumination.

For a full description of this most wonderful time of the year, see Christmas At Historic Houses. For more information, telephone 757.229.1000, or see on-line at www.history.org/history.

The LBJ Ranch

4

Stonewall, Texas

The roster of Historic House Museums in the United States continues to grow. One of the most recent and notable additions is the LBJ Ranch in the Texas Hill Country just west of Austin, the State Capitol. Following the death of former First Lady Mrs. Lady Bird Johnson in 2007, the LBJ Ranch is now maintained by the National Park Service and the house is open to the public as a museum restored to its appearance during the Johnson presidency.

The big white house at the LBJ Ranch was home, then it became the Texas White House, then it was home again—always much beloved by the Johnson family and scene of memorable Christmas celebrations. The late First Lady Mrs. Lyndon Baines Johnson—Lady Bird to all—wrote in her *Lady Bird Johnson, A White House Diary* (Holt, Rinehart and Winston; New York, 1971), "Christmas for the Johnsons always has meant the LBJ Ranch, but during our time when Lyndon was President, we spent two wonderful Christmases at The White House." On those two occasions, she brought a bit of the Ranch to the White House. For Christmas 1967, she brought sprigs of mistletoe to hang over the doorways. For Christmas 1968, she noted: "... *from the ranch, we distributed gifts of jellies and preserves and corn relishes and pickled pears—a beautiful bounty transported north!*"

As President and Mrs. Lyndon Baines Johnson were preparing to leave The White House, Lady Bird stated in her diary, "Christmas of 1968 was a particular time of joy for us. ... We were looking forward to going home to the ranch with its fields of wildflowers to renew us...." Those wildflowers inspired Lady Bird's Beautification Program while she was First Lady of the United States and later the establishing of the Lady Bird Johnson Wildflower Center in Austin, Texas. A small measure of the lasting impact of LBJ Ranch wildflowers, Lady Bird's Beautification Program and the Wildflower

1 At the Texas White House (the LBJ Ranch) antlers attached to the trunk of the mighty oak tree near the front gate are decorated for Christmas. *Photograph by Barbara Justice*

2-3 Under the branches of the magnificent oak, President Lyndon Baines Johnson entertained family, friends, staff and powerful world leaders. *Photograph by Mike Geissinger, courtesy LBJ Library*

The particular beauty of the Texas Hill Country and the sense of home drew President and Mrs. Johnson and their family to the LBJ Ranch for Christmas celebrations.

4

5

6

Center bearing her name is seen in a 2007 award-winning sculpture by master mosaic artist Julie Richey of Dallas, Texas. Julie's amazing *L'Ambasciatrice* (The Ambassadress) sculpture of glass mosaic and *millefiori* beads came about when she was invited to submit a piece to the Lady Bird Johnson Wildflower Center Gala in Austin, Texas. She says, "I researched native Texas wildflowers and began sketching them on the dress form I'd constructed out of rigid wrap, muslin and fabric stiffener (diluted Weldbond) stretched over a mannequin purchased from a children's clothing store that was going out of business." The concept—and those wildflowers vividly drawn in glass tessera—gave Julie's piece the wow factor that won for her the Members' Choice Award at the *Mosaic Arts International Exhibit.*

The particular beauty of the Texas Hill Country and the sense of home drew President and Mrs. Johnson and their family to the LBJ Ranch for Christmas celebrations. President Johnson had purchased the Ranch from an uncle. Elder daughter Lynda Bird Johnson Robb spoke of her father's visiting the house as a boy. "He visited there, and recited poems in the same spot where my girls performed at Christmas. It's a very modest house really—not luxurious."

In 2006, Lynda shared with *Christmas at Historic Houses* her memories of family gatherings (discontinued since her mother's death).

4 In the comfortable living room were three television sets—one for watching all three of the then major channels. *Photograph by Barbara Justice*

5 The refurbished living room looks as it did during the LBJ presidency. Christmas stockings belonging to the late President and Mrs. Johnson hang at the mantel. *Photograph by Barbara Justice*

6 Lady Bird sat before the fireplace at the LBJ Ranch, Christmas 1980, with her grandchildren. (Left to right,) Lyndon Nugent, Jennifer Robb, Nicole Nugent, Claudia Nugent, Lady Bird Johnson, Lucinda Robb, Rebecca Nugent, Catherine Robb. *Photograph by Frank Wolf, courtesy LBJ Library*

7 A needlepoint pillow features the Texas White House. Kits are available in the Gift Shop. *Photograph by Barbara Justice*

8 Family members each had their own hand-made Christmas stocking and all were hung by the mantel with loving care. *Photograph by Frank Wolf, courtesy LBJ Library*

Christmas at the LBJ Ranch is a family tradition that continues. In my 39 years of marriage, we have spent Christmas in our own home only twice. Whenever Christmas places are mentioned, my daughter Lucinda says, "As long as my Nini (Grandmother Lady Bird) is living, we are going to the Ranch for Christmas."

Every family member has a Christmas stocking, and we keep our stockings at the Ranch, where all are hung on the mantel. Stockings for the first two grandchildren were professionally made, but those for later additions to the family have been lovingly handmade by family members. I especially remember the joint efforts of my three daughters who overnight made a Christmas stocking for Lars, who became Lucinda's husband.

I turned the duty of being Santa over to my children, who stuffed the stockings with grocery store scandal sheets (fun reading), lots of candy, and gifts from the dime store. There have been strange gifts—gifts that made us ask, "What will I do with that?" But some have been practical. I remember getting dental floss! Once there were pencils with our names on them. That was very special—no more fussing about which pencil belonged to whom.

Some of our most wonderful memories are of the grandchildren putting on pageants on Christmas Eve. My daughter, Lucinda, directed and produced these sometimes hilarious events. Lyndon Nugent usually ended up being a reindeer, with a sister riding on his back while three younger children played reindeer. Their creative antlers were made of wire clothes-hanger frames, covered with nylon pantyhose stuffed with batting. Once, a niece entered the room in her "sleigh"—a suitcase! Another year, three of the girls were "We Three Kings," wearing caftans from Morocco.

What I love most about the Christmases is that they were times for getting us all together.

9 In one corner of the living room is a piano with a hymnal. *Photograph by Barbara Justice*

10 Scenic wallpaper in muted tones similar to those of the winter grasses beyond the picture window is a gentle backdrop for the oval dining table set for a holiday meal. *Photograph by Barbara Justice*

11-12 Sunny colors enliven the inviting den, a favorite room for Mrs. Johnson. The needlepoint cushion states the case for early arrival for gatherings in this room. *Photograph by Barbara Justice*

13 A handsome cabinet near the den's outside entry door replaces antlers that once served as a hat rack. The stairway leads to second floor bedrooms. *Photograph by Barbara Justice*

11

12

13

"Christmas of 1968 was a particular time of joy for us. … We were looking forward to going home to the ranch with its fields of wildflowers to renew us…."

Do visit the Ranch during the Christmas holiday season. The Office, Dining Room and Living Room will be decorated for Christmas, as they were when the Johnson's were in residence, with President and Mrs. Johnson's Christmas stockings hung at the fireplace. The kitchen is currently being restored and eventually will be open.

16

14

17

15

14-15 Landscapes flank the den door leading to the kitchen. The primitive style painting on the right is by a favorite artist of President Johnson. *Photograph by Barbara Justice*

16 Knotty pine plank walls surround the fireplace in the den. *Photograph by Barbara Justice*

17 On the lounge chair to the left of the fireplace is a needlepoint cushion depicting wildflowers which Mrs. Johnson loved. *Photograph by Barbara Justice*

18

18 Blue Bonnets and Indian Paint Brush at the LBJ Ranch inspired Lady Bird's unique gift to America—her beautification program and the wildflower center named for her. *Photograph by Robert Knudsen, courtesy LBJ Library*

19

19 Dallas-based master mosaic artist Julie Richey's award-winning L'Ambasciatrice, a unique glass mosaic sculpture inspired by Texas wildflowers at the LBJ Ranch, was created for exhibition at the Lady Bird Johnson Wildflower Center, Austin, Texas. *Photograph courtesy Julie Richey*

Visiting LBJ Country

The "Texas White House" and the many historic sites associated with the Johnson family is the very good reason why this part of the famed Texas Hill Country is called LBJ Country. One can glimpse the life of LBJ by visiting various sites, including:

- *The Johnson Settlement nearby, where the cabin and buildings which belonged to LBJ's grandfather have been restored.*
- *The re-created home where LBJ was born—now on the LBJ Ranch.*
- *President Johnson's boyhood home*
- *LBJ Historical National Historical Park in Johnson City (near Stonewall).*
- *The 600-acre LBJ Ranch. The centerpiece of the Ranch, the spacious Texas White House sets beneath the giant oak tree where LBJ visited with family, friends, neighbors, and visiting heads of state. Near the house is the carport filled with cars used by the President, his family and visitors to the Ranch.*

In mid-December an Annual Tree Lighting ceremony takes place at the Lyndon Baines Johnson State Park and Historical Site. The community-wide event features carolers, a live nativity, Santa Claus, a candlelight and lamp-lit 1900 Sauer-Beckmann Living History Farm, and a special nighttime holiday tour of the LBJ National Historical Park and Texas White House. Traditionally, members of the LBJ family attend.

Christmas at the LBJ Ranch and other Historic Houses across the nation remind us of the contributions to our nation of lives well lived.

21

22

23

20 A portrait of the late President Lyndon Baines Johnson hangs above the fireplace in the ranch-house office he used following his presidency. *Photograph by Barbara Justice*

21 To the right of the fireplace is a Barcalounger recliner with the Seal of the President of The United States of America—and a cushion that expresses a very personal sentiment. *Replicas of the cushion are for sale in the Gift Shop. Photograph by Barbara Justice*

22 Lady Bird Johnson opens Christmas gifts near the ceiling-high Christmas tree in the office in 1965. *Photograph by Frank Wolf, courtesy LBJ Library*

23 The late President Johnson's desk faces the fireplace in his ranch home office. A ceiling-high tree towers above the furnishings, setting the tone for the season of family festivity.

Oldfields-Lilly

5

Indianapolis, Indiana

"At Oldfields, Christmas decorations take their cues from the styles popular from the 1920s through the 1940s," says Bradley Brooks, Director. A holiday visit to this gracious home is not a journey into a distant past, but a privileged, leisurely look at lives well lived in the 20th century.

The 22-room country house in the French château style takes its name from the farmland on which the estate is sited. Oldfields was designed by architect Lewis Ketcham Davis, and built in the early 1900s for Hugh McKennan Landon, an executive with the Indianapolis Water company, and his wife, Suzette Davis Landon, the architect's sister.

During the 1920s, Landon and his second wife, Jessie Walker Landon, began to develop the grounds at Oldfields. They hired the Olmsted Brothers landscape firm of Brookline, Massachusetts (successors to the firm founded by Frederick Law Olmsted who designed New York City's Central Park) to develop the property. Percival Gallagher of Olmsted created a classic allée or tree-lined vista, re-designed the formal garden and did other extensive work to create a classic country estate.

The Winter sun rises on the elegant alee—a spacious ornamental-tree-lined pathway—pouring light on a serene holiday snowscape at the French château-style Oldfields-Lilly House. *All photographs courtesy Indianapolis Museum of Art (IMA), Oldfields-Lilly House & Gardens*

A holiday visit to this gracious home is not a journey into a distant past, but a privileged, leisurely look at lives well lived in the 20th century.

The Lilly House

In 1932, J.K. Lilly, Jr. and his wife Ruth purchased Oldfields. They hired architect Frederick Wallick to make numerous changes in the house.

Wallick improved the façade's symmetry by relocating the off-center entrance and by repositioning a number of dormer windows. Rooms were altered to improve both function and appearance. After relocating the entry, the mansion's front door opened into the Great Hall, the largest room in the Lilly home.

A love of literature and a passion for rare books inspired Lilly to begin a collection in the 1920s. A handsome new walnut-paneled library in the Georgian style replaced what had been a sunroom at the south end of the house to accommodate Lilly's growing rare books collection. Over thirty years' time, the collection grew to some 20,000 volumes of books and 17,000 manuscripts. Lilly donated his collection in 1954 to Indiana University.

The Game Room, originally fitted with gothic-style oak woodwork and shoulder-height bookcases was re-paneled in birds-eye maple. New floor-to-ceiling bookcases added shelving for books. A marble fireplace was added.

In the 1950s, bookcases were covered over and the walls painted to create display space for paintings and the game room became the morning room.

The drawing room, smaller than the great hall, was used for more intimate gatherings. Moldings framed panels of hand-painted Chinese wallpaper that created a delightful background for furnishings including a type of player piano for musical entertainment. In the 1950s, fashion had changed and so did the drawing room. Moldings and paper panels were removed and the walls were covered in silk.

The Dining Room with its west-facing windows was paneled in mahogany during the Landons' time. The Lillys brightened the room with a new paint treatment.

The Kitchen was updated in the 1930s with new cabinets and linoleum floors and countertops.

1 In the evening, as the last light of day fades, festive holiday lighting welcomes guests to gala evening events during the high holiday season.

2 In the lively stair hall, amaryllis, poinsettias, and a lavish garland of fruit and flowers fill the air with the scents of Christmas.

The loggia—a common feature of country houses, providing an easy transition from house to grounds—was fitted with wicker and painted wood furniture during the Landons' residency. The Lillys commissioned Canadian muralist Douglas Riseborough to create landscape murals on the walls in the 1950s. This area remains as it was in the 1950s, while the rest of the house has been restored to its 1930s look.

An 18th-century Italian looking glass reflects the beautifully bedecked Christmas tree that stands in the adjoining Great Hall.

During the Lilly family's long residency at Oldfields, J.K. Lilly, Jr. was active in his grandfather's pharmaceutical firm Eli Lilly and Company, and was instrumental in establishing firms to market the parent company's products internationally. At the same time, Lilly expanded his personal interests beyond rare books to collect stamps and gold coins. His gold coin collection became one of the largest in the world and was acquired after his death by the Smithsonian Institution. His stamp collection, also one of the world's largest, was sold at auction after Lilly's death.

The drawing room, with its exquisitely hand-painted Chinese-motif wallpaper, needs little other decoration. Pots of bamboo adorned with origami cranes adds just the right touch.

Ruth Lilly and J.K. Lilly Jr. died in 1965 and 1966 respectively. In 1967 their children, Ruth Lilly and J.K. Lilly III, donated the estate to the Art Institute of Indianapolis, which established its new campus on the site. The renamed Indianapolis Museum of Art opened its new building to the public in 1970. Oldfields-Lilly House & Gardens is now a National Historic Landmark.

The Dining Room is furnished with antique Chippendale chairs and other English antiques from the late 18th century. A silver-and-crystal epergne filled with shining Christmas ornaments serves as a stunning centerpiece for the mahogany dining table.

Mount Clare

6

Baltimore, Maryland

In 18th century America, holiday decoration was more restrained than in the exuberant 19th century, but celebration was none-the-less festive. At Mount Clare, the 1760 colonial Georgian home built by Charles Carroll, Barrister, one of Maryland's leading patriots, one can experience the splendor of the earlier era surrounded by original architecture, furnishings, art and artifacts. Beginning early in December, when elegant interiors are filled with wreathes, boxwood trees, roping and holly, the public is invited to enjoy events filled with music, singing, and foods from the period.

Early Years

Mount Clare, a classic Georgian house was begun in 1756. It is built of soft pink brick—probably made on Carroll's plantation, Georgia, site of the owner's new country home. In the classical style created by the architect Palladio, the main body of the house is flanked by wings connected to the central portion by hyphens.

Descriptions of the house note that interior walls are of fire-resistant plaster that resemble wood (which has never been replaced) and that heavy plaster cornices join walls and ceilings.

Double doors open into a central passageway. Immediately inside the door on the right is the Barrister's study. Opposite the study is a handsome staircase that leads to the second floor. Straight ahead, a passage way leads to a large parlor where original portraits by Charles Willson Peale, whose training as an artist was supported by the Barrister and his friends. Opposite the parlor (adjacent to the stair) is the dining room or eating parlor, an innovation in the 18th century when common practice called for setting up tables wherever the family wished. On the second floor beyond a gracious landing are three bedrooms.

1-2 In the dawn's early light and evening's last rays, Mount Clare, with its flanking dependencies and Palladian-style window, is a shining example of the mature Georgian architectural style. Baltimore's oldest surviving colonial home and first museum house, it was the Carroll's summer home, the centerpiece of an 800-acre estate now just minutes from the city's inner harbor.

3 Entry gate pillars crowned with the Carroll shield wear Christmas wreaths.

At Mount Clare, the 1760 colonial Georgian home built by Charles Carroll, Barrister, one of Maryland's leading patriots, one can experience the splendor of the earlier era surrounded by original architecture, furnishings, art and artifacts.

4-5 Above the mantel in the dining room, a portrait of Barrister Charles Carroll by John Hesselius (in its original 1763 frame) presides over a trove of treasures in silver and porcelain. The silver epergne centerpiece was made in London in 1763. Nanking blue-and-white porcelain custard cups (with tops) can be seen on the table and mantel. Plates in the cupboard and on the 1815 Baltimore-made mahogany table are Imari-style Chinese export porcelain c. 1760-1770. *All photographs courtesy Mount Clare Museum House*

6

7

6-7 Charles Wilson Peale, famed portraitist of George Washington, Thomas Jefferson and Charles Carroll, painted portraits of Carroll's wife and of his niece, Mary Clare Maccubbin, with her daughter. *All photographs courtesy Mount Clare Museum House*

8 Setting on the mantel in the Dining Room Chamber (Margaret's bedroom) is a French clock that was owned by Joshua Barney, a Baltimorean a famed naval officer during the Revolutionary War and the War of 1812. The red wing chair is in the Hepplewhite style, c. 1785. The portable rosewood lap desk is c. 1815.

9 Pegasus, the rocking horse, stands before the parlor chamber (the Barrister's bedroom) fireplace—which has one of only two original Georgian-era fireplace surrounds (all other mantels are Federal Period Adamesque style). The Chippendale-style side chair was made in Philadelphia in 1765.

10 The clock on the mantle in the Study depicting George Washington was made in 1805 by Dubue of Paris, France.

11

12

Throughout the house are many furnishings and artifacts that belonged to the Carrolls. Outstanding examples include Mrs. Carroll's white and gold furniture of the Louis XV period in the living room, c. 1760-70, Chinese export Imari porcelain in the dining room, two original Georgian era fireplace surrounds, 1785 Sheffield silver candlesticks, pair of 1790 Hepplewhite card tables, a decanter and glassware traveling set owned by the Barrister in 1765. And, there is much, much more.

Later Years

After Charles Carroll's death, Mrs. Carroll moved from Annapolis to make Mount Clare her permanent home. When Mrs. Carroll died in 1817, because there were no surviving children, the property went to a nephew, James Maccubbin, who assumed the Carroll surname. In 1870, Carroll heirs leased the house to the Baltimore Scheutzen Association and in 1890, sold the house and 20 acres to the City of Baltimore Park Commission, which expanded the property to 36 acres and hired the Olmsted Brothers Architects to make improvements to the park lands in 1904. Over the years, changes had been made to the buildings. In 1917, the Colonial Dames of America in the State of Maryland assumed custody of the house to manage and operate it as Maryland's first Museum House. It was designated a National Historic Landmark in 1971. Today, Mount Clare is a fine example of life in Maryland more than two centuries ago when Christmas was the height of the winter social season.

11-12 In the kitchen is a spinning or "walking" wheel, traditional fruit centerpiece ready to transport to the dining room, and a table filled with dishes typical of the time when the Carrolls were at home at Mount Clare.

Samuel Cupples

7

St. Louis, Missouri

MEET ME IN SAINT LOUIS—an inspired idea any time of the year—is an especially good idea when plans include a visit to the historic Samuel Cupples House, a rare example of residential Richardsonian Romanesque style. An ideal time to visit this extraordinary house is at Christmas time, when the house is beautifully decorated in anticipation of Santa's annual St. Louis visit. Plan to be present at the annual Christmas tree lighting ceremony described by Neil Metzger, Museum Assistant, Galleries and Museums of Saint Louis University:

Father Maurice McNamee was the Jesuit priest responsible for saving and subsequently refurnishing the 42-room Romanesque mansion known as the Historic Samuel Cupples House on the campus of Saint Louis University. Prior to his death in February 2007, at the age of 97, Father McNamee was the guest of honor at the Cupples House Christmas tree lighting.

In honor of Father Mac, the holiday tree lighting continues and the historic mansion that he saved and restored is resplendent in its holiday finery. After the tree lighting, the celebration continues with a choral performance in the grand hall by the members of the Saint Louis University Fine and Performing Arts department. Faculty, staff, students and members of the community are encouraged to bring a gift of clothing to benefit the parish help center of Saint Francis Xavier (The College) Church, also located on the campus of Saint Louis University.

While The Historic Samuel Cupples House welcomes guests throughout the year, the holidays are a special time to visit and enjoy the art, ambiance and holiday décor found throughout the three floors of the magnificent mansion that Father McNamee restored and renovated with his heart and soul.

1 An annual Christmas Tree Lighting Ceremony launches the Holiday Season at the Samuel Cupples House at St. Louis University, where a brilliantly decorated Christmas Tree in the Reception Room greets visitors. *Photographs courtesy Samuel Cupples House at St. Louis University*

2 A photograph taken of the Music Room shortly after the Cupples moved into their new home in 1890, shows an eclectic combination of furnishings typically found throughout the house. Christmas décor adds lively good cheer.

3 The railing of the Minstrel Balcony which overlooks the main hall and faces the Reception Room, is decorated with evergreen garlands and ribbon.

1

1 Front view of the Samuel Cupples House by architect H. H. Richardson show the monumental Romanesque Revival style usually reserved for institutions.

2 The massive double front door with its ornate iron hinges wears greenery and ribbons for Christmas.

3 Greenery adds robust holiday cheer to the handsome Foyer with its walls of rich, dark paneling.

Inside, Tiffany-styled windows bathed the home with beautiful light that played upon the rich woods expertly carved by craftsmen brought from England by Cupples.

4 "The Holy Family," by an artist of the Bolognese school is one of the important paintings—including Northern and Italian Renaissance artists' works brought to St. Louis in 1845 by Jesuit missionary Peter De Smer, S.J.—which comprise the significant St. Louis University art collection.

5 Copper gilt beams and a gilded medallion highlight the Conservatory ceiling. The original glass ceiling leaked so badly the Samuel Cupples' grandchildren called the Conservatory "the wet room."

The fact that the house stands today may be considered something of a miracle. In 1919 the Brotherhood of Railroad Telegraphers bought the house to use as their corporate headquarters, then in 1946, Saint Louis University purchased the house for use as classrooms and a student center. In 1964, the University planned to demolish the aging Cupples House, but Father McNamee, who was on the professorial staff, championed the history and architectural significance of the building. Neil Metzger recounts the history of this remarkable structure.

Romanesque Revival buildings of the late-nineteenth century repudiated the fussy neo-gothic twists and turns of Victorian architecture. Rounded arches set upon short columns, complicated roof lines and soaring towers conveyed to the public a sense of stability and strength that made the style attractive to civic groups and churches.

Romanesque Revival was rarely the choice for individuals, however. As imposing as a building's look was the financial cost of masonry construction. Such buildings also imposed a great burden for the interior where close attention to detail was required to minimize the foreboding effects of substantial construction. A typical Romanesque structure was more often a church or city hall rather than a private home. Yet Romanesque was the style Samuel Cupples chose for his house on West Pine Boulevard, a house to be built upon the highest ground in the city of St. Louis. Purple sandstone from Colorado was laid upon the pink foundation granite of southern Missouri.

Inside, Tiffany-styled windows bathed the home with beautiful light that played upon the rich woods expertly carved by craftsmen brought from England by Cupples.

The exterior was just as richly detailed. Expert stone masons chiseled an intriguing feast for the eye. Delicate vines twist along balconies while strange beings – mythical animals and dwarves – hug the rainspouts and gutters. Rounded towers clad in copper and fantastical chimneys pierce the sky, shaping one of the most interesting roofs in the city of St. Louis.

Mr. Cupples' house was designed by Thomas Annan. Construction began in 1888 and the home became the residence of the Cupples family in 1890. There are 42 rooms in Cupples House and twenty-two fireplaces. Entertainments and galas, though no dancing, were held in the formal rooms of the first floor while the second and third floors were reserved to the family. In 1904, a conservatory was added to the rear of the house.

In 1919, Samuel Cupples' heirs sold the home to the Brotherhood of Railroad Telegraphers who used the building as their national headquarters. In 1946, the Telegraphers sold the house to Saint Louis University. The university used the building as a student union and many Saint Louis University graduates remember Mr. Cupples' house as Chouteau House.

In 1973, Father Maurice McNamee, S.J. took on the task of restoring the house to its original appearance. A century of coal dust and city grime was removed, once again revealing the rich colors of the stone exterior. Years of paint were removed revealing original wall papers. The effect of such dedicated labor and support resulted in the placement of the Samuel Cupples House on the National Historic Register in 1977.

The Samuel Cupples House serves also as a gallery for Saint Louis University. Priceless art, including oil paintings brought to the St. Louis frontier by Father Peter De Smet, S.J., adorn the walls of the house. American decorative art, particularly Steuben and Tiffany glass, is featured at Cupples House.

For your next Christmas, do accept the invitation by the staff of St. Louis University to meet in St. Louis—at the historic Samuel Cupples House!

Hazelwood

8

Greenbay, Wisconsin

Christmas at Hazelwood promises all the thrills of an authentic Victorian Christmas—and it happens in Wisconsin's scenic Brown County. To return to the Victorian era, with its love of lavish decoration and convivial gatherings of family and friends, makes the winter holidays the most wonderful time of a glorious year.

Morgan Lewis Martin came to Wisconsin—then a Territory and considered the northern frontier—as a young graduate of Hamilton College with a degree in law. He left behind his stately boyhood home, Greystone Manor, in Martinsburg (named for his father, General Walter Martin) in New York State. He established his law practice in Green Bay, became a successful businessman, and devoted much of his life to Wisconsin politics.

Martin was a Wisconsin delegate to the United States Congress from 1845 to 1847. He was president of the 1848 convention in Madison that drafted Wisconsin's constitution. His home, Hazelwood, is on the National Register of Historic Places. Legend is that the Wisconsin Constitution was written from conversations around the table that remains in place in the Hazelwood dining room.

Martin built Hazelwood in 1837, for his bride, Elizabeth Smith Martin. The architectural design—based on Greystone Manor—is credited to Joseph Jackson, a family friend. At this comfortable home, in an area now known as the Astor Historic District, the Martins raised their five children.

Hazelwood is the home of Morgan Lewis Martin, an important Wisconsin politician who helped frame the Wisconsin Constitution. *Photographs courtesy the Hazelwood Historic House & Museum and the Brown County Historical Society*

Legend is that the Wisconsin Constitution was written from conversations around the table that remains in place in the Hazelwood dining room.

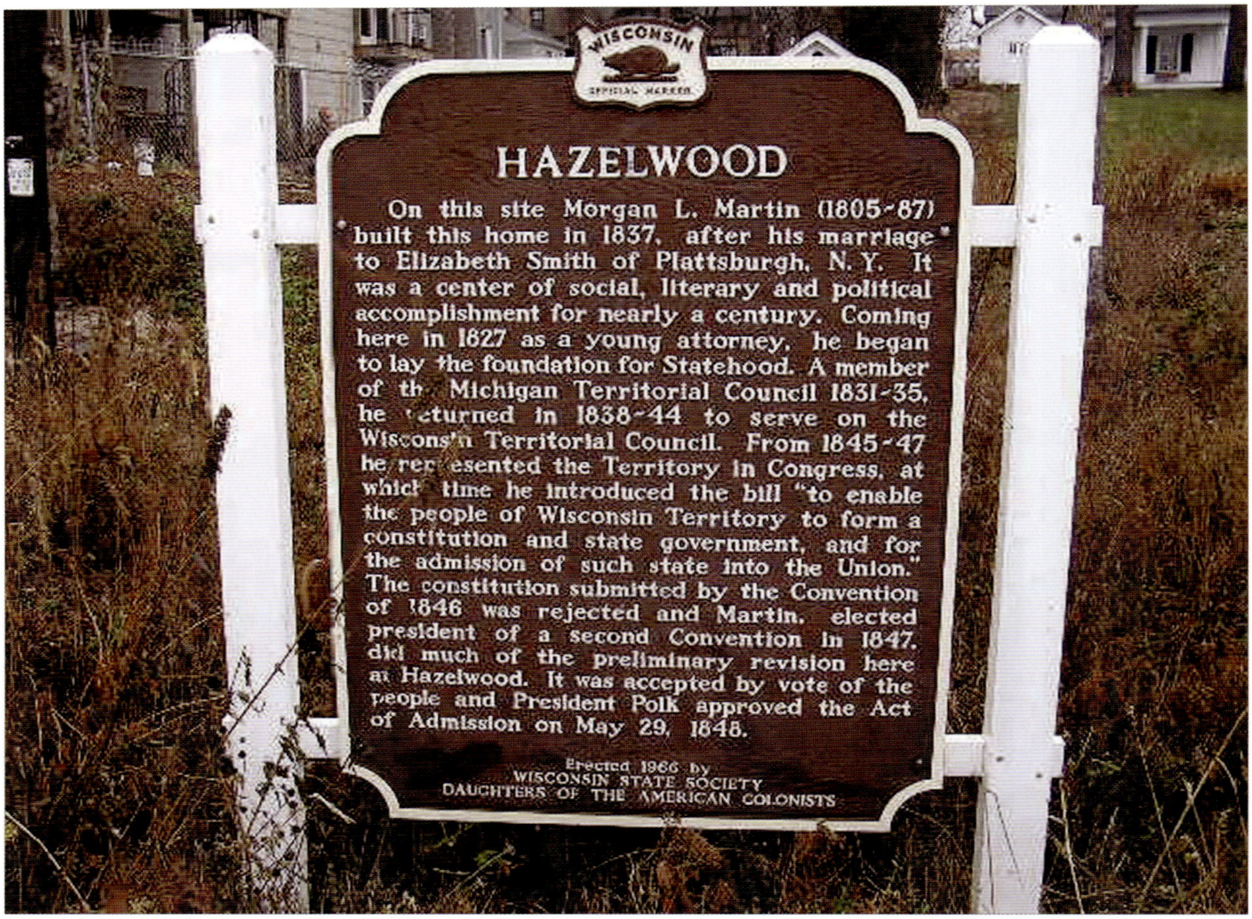

To walk into this Greek Revival style home—charming in its elegant simplicity, romantic in its timeliness—is to step into history.

A long hallway runs from the front of the house to the rear, originally considered the main entrance. The sitting room was used for family gatherings and family members read and did craft work here. The dining room did double duty as a place for serious political discussions. In the early days, meals were prepared on a cooking hearth in the cellar. A summer kitchen stood adjacent to the main house. By 1890, the southern wing of the building housed a Victorian kitchen. This wing was demolished in the 1930s, but has been reconstructed and the 1890s kitchen restored.

On the second floor only the Master Bedroom had a fireplace. Other bedrooms were fitted with stoves to ward off the extreme cold of Wisconsin winters.

Reading and writing were important to the Martins. Mrs. Martin, who was fluent in three languages, documented her life in diaries described as meticulously kept. In late life, she wrote historical articles.

In 1966, the Wisconsin State Society Daughters of the American Colonists erected a sign recognizing Morgan Lewis Martin's contribution to Wisconsin Statehood and Hazelwood as an important state landmark.

The youngest Martin daughter, Deborah, authored (with her sister, Sarah Greene Martin, and Ella Hoes Neville) *Historic Green Bay*. She was one of the first to work toward preserving Hazelwood and to photograph the interiors.

Today, Hazelwood is owned and operated as a museum by the Brown County Historical Society. According to Curator of Interpretation Sally Enloe, visitor comments routinely include phrases like "beautiful house," "excellent tour," and "well maintained." Hazelwood truly is a vital link to Wisconsin history past, present and future.

The decorative parlor was where the family gathered for craftwork and reading, while in the nearby dining room, Wisconsin's potential statehood was discussed and its new constitution written at the dining room table.

The Deere-Wiman House and Butterworth Center

9

Moline, Illinois

Two homes for the holidays! One is Butterworth Center, the 1892 home of the granddaughter of John Deere (the Vermont blacksmith who made life easier and more productive for American farmers), Katherine Butterworth and her husband, William. The other is Katherine's childhood home, the Deere-Wiman House, a magnificent 1872 home built by Charles Deere, John's son.

A Christmas visit to Butterworth Center and the Deere-Wiman House is an extraordinary journey into the 19th century when Christmas was enriched by fine objects, but made richer still with meanings for the heart and lessons for the future.

Executive Director Susan Staack says, "Long before fall's chilly nights nip the last leaf from the golden chestnut on the lawn, the Butterworth Center and Deere-Wiman House staff starts making plans to welcome thousands of guests to our 19th century Christmas, held each year on the first Sunday in December. Our goal is to help families make memories to add to those from a century of joyous Christmases already celebrated at Butterworth Center and Deere-Wiman House. As you can see, the spirit of generosity and community involvement has been our focus for over 50 years."

According to Ms. Staack, long before many charitable organizations established their own outreach programs, every year Mrs. Butterworth secretly bought Christmas gifts for the ladies who lived at Oak Glen Nursing Home. Mrs. Pattie Southall Wiman, the last Deere family member to reside in Deere-Wiman House (until her death in 1976), assumed "Santa's" duties at Oak Glen after Mrs. Butterworth's death in 1953. "Because of Katherine Butterworth's legacy of generosity, we still carry on her traditions of hospitality and service to the community she loved," says Ms. Staack.

1 Massive iron gates hung with colorful wreaths greet visitors to Butterworth Center (known as Hillcrest), the 25,000 square foot home of John Deere's granddaughter Katherine and her husband, William Butterworth. *Photographs courtesy Butterworth Center & Deere-Wiman House*

2-3 Evergreens and dried hydrangeas and other flowers from the gardens provide natural materials for holiday decorations. In the richly paneled entry hall, simple evergreen garlands outline stone-trimmed doorways. A peek into the 25 x 50 sq. ft. library shows the ornate mantel decorations.

A Christmas visit to Butterworth Center and the Deere-Wiman House is an extraordinary journey into the 19th century when Christmas was enriched by fine objects, but made richer still with meanings for the heart and lessons for the future.

The Beginning of Butterworth Center

The story of Butterworth Center and Deere-Wiman House—two very different, but related houses—begins with the story of John Deere, the Vermont blacksmith who decided he must leave the depressed state of Vermont and go west. Leaving his wife and family (who would join him later) he set out with few resources for Grand Detour, Illinois, which had been settled by a fellow Vermont native. The need for a blacksmith was so great that within two days of his arrival, he set up a forge and was in business. The history of the growth of the John Deere & Company is a fascinating story of the growth of a company whose leader insisted on the highest quality—never cutting corners or slacking, but providing the best, first of himself, then of his products. In a sense, his story is the story of America's agricultural industry. It is also one of the growth of a family, and two great houses—the Deere-Wiman House and Butterworth Center.

5

The Deere-Wiman House

John Deere's son, Charles, built the Deere-Wiman House (originally called Overlook) in 1872, for his wife, Mary Little Dickinson Deere, and their daughters Anna and Katherine. The Swiss style villa sets on seven acres on a hilltop overlooking the city of Moline and the family business, then the John Deere Plow Works. Inside, it featured the latest technology, including indoor plumbing. By 1899, an elevator was installed and a central vacuum system was added. Four generations of Deere descendants lived at Overlook, which is about 15,000 square feet. Other changes included removing a fireplace wall between a morning room and parlor to create a large formal living room, enlarging the music room to accommodate a pipe organ, and converting the porch into a conservatory with a glass-domed ceiling, and then later into a breakfast room. Despite its rich architectural features and fine furnishings, Overlook was first and foremost a family home and comfortably furnished, distinctly decorated bedrooms and casual living spaces reflect that. A child's playhouse reminds visitors that generations of children were at home at Overlook.

6

4 In the Music Room, Christmas trees in Oriental porcelain containers are decorated with swags of dried roses.

5 A garden-grown evergreen rope decorates the mantel in the Green Room.

6 Soft pink poinsettias gently echo the colors of the French Room walls in the Deere-Wiman home.

7

The Butterworth Center

In 1892, John Deere's granddaughter, Katherine (daughter of Charles Deere who had succeeded his father as head of the Deere & Company) married William Butterworth, Charles built Butterworth Center (known as Hillcrest) as a wedding present for Katherine, and her new husband joined Deere & Company as an assistant buyer. Armed with a degree from Lehigh University and a law degree from the National University of Law School in Washington, William became president of the company in 1907.

Over the years, William and Katherine Butterworth expanded the house several times. Eventually, it was approximately triple its original size. In 1909, both living and dining rooms were enlarged. A 26-rank pipe organ was installed in the new living room area. New French doors in the dining room opened onto a new patio. In 1925, a carriage entrance was replaced with

a ground-level port cochere. Here, arriving guests entered the lower level Oak Room and climbed an impressive staircase to the first floor foyer. Above the port cochere, the new library was designed around a 52-by 30-foot ceiling painting on canvas from Venice, Italy created in the 16th century. Architectural elements and furnishings reflected the grand style. Several pieces of furniture original to the home remain. The spectacular library is only one of the rooms and elements designed to fascinate.

7 One block from Butterworth Center, wreaths on the iron gates at the entry to the seven-acre Deere-Wiman estate welcome visitors to Katherine Deere Butterworth's childhood home known as Overlook.

8 At the 1872 Deere-Wiman House, a porte cochere provides protection from inclement weather for arriving guests.

9 Swags of lavish greenery enlivens a mantel in the Living Room.

Chief Vann House

10

Chatsworth, Georgia

"You are invited to a Cherokee Christmas by Candlelight."

This singular annual event revisits the gracious brick mansion of Chief James Vann, site of the first celebration of Christmas within the Cherokee Nation. The year was 1805.

The story of how Christmas came to the Cherokees is fascinating. Chief Vann—in his day one of the wealthiest men in the western hemisphere—gave Moravian missionaries from Salem, North Carolina property just east of his home. There they opened the Moravian "Springplace Mission," the first mission and school for the Cherokee Indian Tribe.

By 1807, Christmas had become a grand observance by both the Moravians and the Cherokee. A cedar tree was decorated with popcorn, cranberries, cookies, paper chains, spice bags, and Bible verse cards. An entry in the Springplace Mission diary for December 21, 1805 reads:

> *Today we went three miles in our cart with our pupils to fetch a Christmas tree.*

1 Luminaries line walkways of the Georgian-style mansion built near Chatsworth, Georgia by the wealthy Scot-Cherokee Chief James Vann. President James Monroe called on Chief Vann's 20-year-old son, Joseph, who inherited his father's estate, at this house. *Photographs by Bob Busby, courtesy Chief Vann House Historic Site*

2 Moravian missionaries from Salem, North Carolina brought the Christian religion to the Cherokee in 1801, and a Christmas ceremony was held in this house in 1805. A wreath in the window was a symbol of welcome.

Christmas was celebrated with religious services, singing, exchanging of gifts, and a traditional Moravian "love feast."

Following is a selected passage from the Mission diary:

December 24-25, 1807-1830:

In the evening we our pupils, and Mrs. Vann celebrated Christmas. Brother Gambold had decorated the halls with flowers, green boughs, and an illuminated painting. After lighted candles had been distributed, Brother Gambold wished all present God's blessings. All the Indian children received presents and cloth for new shirts woven by our pupil Betsy Busby. One-hundred-and-fifty came to join us in prayer at the manger of the Christ child. The service opened with the song What Good News the Angels Bring, followed by a short walk for the children. William Hicks repeated what had been said for those who could not understand English. In addition, he read from the 25th chapter of Matthew and from John 10 in their language. At the love feast we and the children sang a joyful Hosanna and other Christmas verses.

3 Soft light, a finely set table, and good food made the dining room a popular gathering place.

4 The living room focal point is the colorfully decorated, picturesque mantel.

Chief Vann House

James Vann, son of a Scottish trader named Vann and a Cherokee woman named Waw-Li, was born in 1768, in Spring Place in Georgia. A member of the Cherokee Triumvirate and town chief of the Cherokee, James Vann built his stately brick Georgian style mansion on his plantation in what is now Murray County, Georgia. It consisted of hundreds of acres of land worked by 110 slaves. One of the oldest remaining structures in Northwest Georgia, the house sets on a hill west of Chatsworth, Georgia, with a commanding view of the Cohutta Mountains which are about ten miles easterly.

In addition to his plantation, James Vann owned many taverns, but it was in a tavern owned by a man named Buffington that Vann was shot to death in 1809.

The Chief Vann house passed to Vann's eldest son, Joseph, who, at age 20, received a visit from President James Monroe. Called "Rich Joe," Joseph proved to be a shrewd businessman able to expand his family's considerable wealth. When Joseph hired a white man to manage his plantation, he unwittingly broke a Georgia law that forbade such a thing without a permit. This breach allowed the Georgia Guard to try to take possession of the house. Similar attempts by others are the stuff of legend. It is reported that after the Land Lottery of 1832, a man named Spencer Riley tried to take the house. In an ensuing battle between Riley and the Guard, the famous cantilevered "floating" steps of the house were damaged by a burning log. The damage is obvious to this day.

Another tale involves the imprisoning of John Howard Payne (composer of *Home Sweet Home*) in the house, who was charged with supporting Cherokee claims over those of Georgia.

Finally, Chief Vann joined other Cherokee on the infamous "Trail of Tears." The much-fought-over house passed though many owners until local citizens held a fund-raiser and purchased the house in 1952. By that time, the roof had come off, leaving the remarkable cantilevered staircase unprotected from the ravages of the elements. This group of concerned citizens donated the house to the Georgia Historical Commission, which began its restoration in 1953.

In 1958, the Chief Vann House, restored to is original grandeur, was opened to the public, and its history—warts and all (that is, good and bad)—is preserved for posterity.

5 A Christmas tree stands at the entry of a bedroom furnished with a handsome four-poster bed.

6 Candles light the desktop at the Chief Vann House.

Federal Hill
My Old Kentucky Home

11

Bardstown, Kentucky

Being at home for the holidays is idyllic—especially when home is Federal Hill, inspiration for Stephen Foster's memorable melody *My Old Kentucky Home*.

Candlelight tours of Federal Hill during the Holidays conjure words and music to *My Old Kentucky Home*, and visions of life at the handsome home built between 1810 and 1818 by Judge John Rowan, a protégé of Henry Clay, and former Congressman and U.S. Senator.

An enduring legend has it that the sentimental ballad was composed by Yankee Stephen Foster after a visit to the home of his cousin, Judge Rowan, in 1850 (or 1852). Inspired by southern hospitality (and perhaps by Federal Hill's slave quarters, some suggest) Foster penned the minstrel tune. It became Kentucky's state song, sung as an anthem before the start of the annual Kentucky Derby (one of the three horse races known collectively as the Triple Crown). At any rate, the song, the house, the park surrounding it, and Bardstown are well known and much visited.

Visitors to Christmas events at the house in Year 2006 found the interiors much changed. Thanks to an anonymous donation of close to one million dollars, once-formal Federal style rooms have been re-done. Gone is the "quiet good taste" of the refined Federal style. In its place is the vigorous Victorian style décor that would have been popular during Foster's visit. That, of course, means vivid colors and strong patterns, usually mixed together with pattern-on-pattern glee.

The new materials—wall coverings, colors, and patterns—were chosen by Curator Ron Langdon, restoration consultant Kevin Hereford, and Brooks Howard of the state Department of Parks historic sites and museums. The explanation for the palm-tree-patterned paper chosen for the dining room is that it refers to Rowan's tour as U.S. *charge d'affaires* to the Kingdom of the Two Sicilies (comprised of Sicily and Naples) in the 1840s.

1 Federal Hill (called My Old Kentucky Home) was built by Judge John Rowan, a relative of Stephen Foster, who may have been inspired to compose "My Old Kentucky Home" following a visit to the house. *Photographs courtesy Federal Hill, My Old Kentucky Home State Park*

2 During the holidays, costumed re-enacters guide visitors on tours of freshly decorated room.

3-4 The dining room—with its stylish wallpapered walls—is simply decorated for the holidays, with focus on the sideboard's elaborate display of fruits and greens.

So, while the December sun may or may not be shining brightly on My Old Kentucky Home, indoors the Christmas season mood is one of great good cheer.

5

6

Selections for other rooms may have less direct connection with the Rowan family, but they do typify the Victorian era that witnessed the birth of Federal Hill and the penning of Foster's memorable music. So memorable that visitors to Federal Hill cannot see a statue of its owner, Judge Rowan, but can see a bronze statute of Foster, described as "seated, barefoot, and apparently composing…."

The house is decorated for Christmas as it would have been in the Victorian area; that is, with a gloriously bedecked tree (chockablock with ornaments), beribboned garlands, and greenery galore. So, while the December sun may or may not be shining brightly on My Old Kentucky Home, indoors the Christmas season mood is one of great good cheer.

7

10

9

8

5 Costumed guides reenact Christmas past at Federal Hill.

6 A stylized Christmas tree with handmade ornaments was typical of the Victorian era which was wild about ornamentation and decoration.

7 Large-scale wallpaper patterns generally featured flowers. This romantic Gothic style window pattern is unusual and beautifully colors in French blues and greys.

8–9 Bedrooms are not always decorated for the holidays, nor do they need any decoration in order to be more beautiful. Distinctive color palettes, intriguing pattern play, and handsome furniture create memorable settings year 'round.

10 Judge Rowan's "home office" was not in the "big house," but was a building apart.

Marshal's House at the Jail

12

Independence, Missouri

When the citizens of Jackson County, Missouri, built a new jail—this time of native limestone—they were thoughtful enough to build a new residence for the Marshal as well. Actually, according to Steve Noll, Director of the Jackson County Historical Society which runs the historic site, the jail was an extension of the Marshal's house and not visible from the street. "The jail museum can be accurately described as the first historic preservation project (1959) in Jackson County, and stands today as practically unchanged from its original construction. The 'new addition' dates from 1903," he says.

Of the two structures—Marshal's house and jail—the residence was decidedly the more elegant, a Federal style, two-story brick home. It was also a more desirable place to spend Christmas.

Today, it is one of three historic houses included in a traditional Twilight Tour that takes place the first Sunday of December. Costumed guides recreate living tableaus of life in Independence when it was an important stop along the much-traveled Santa Fe Trail.

Inside the Marshal's house and down the entry hallway on the right is the parlor, furnished as it was in the 19th century. The piano once belonged to a woman who was imprisoned in the jail next door, under the infamous Order 11, which intended to rid the area of Southern sympathizers. For those who did not play the piano, there was a music box that played ten songs. There are two portraits in this formal sitting room. One is of Clay County's first judge, Judge Chevis. The other is of Mrs. Eliza Waldo, wife of Dr. David Waldo, whose portrait at one time hung above the mantel. Legend has it that after the house had become a museum, each morning volunteer staffers would discover Mrs. Waldo's portrait mysteriously on the floor. They would re-hang it, only to have to repeat the process the following day. Finally,

1-2 A plaque and traditional wreaths and greenery welcome holiday visitors to the Marshal's 1859 Federal-style home in Independence, Missouri. Next door is the jail, which once housed (in style and comfort) one of the infamous James Brothers, who dined with his jailer! *Photographs by Janeen Aggen, courtesy of Independence, Missouri Tourism*

3 Garlands, wreaths, and ropes of greenery brightened with red ribbons decorate the graceful stair and brighten the entry hall at the Marshal's house.

The jail next door has even stronger ties, since it housed the infamous and very popular Frank James—in style!

Mantels are simply decorated as they would have been when the Marshal's home was built. In the parlor, with its handsome scroll-arm exposed wood frame Victorian sofa, refreshments are arranged on a tea table. German settlers introduced the custom of the tabletop Christmas tree.

Dr. Waldo's portrait was moved to the upstairs hallway. Mrs. Waldo's portrait remained in place on the parlor wall.

A curiosity is an oval hair-wreath picture—with flowers made from the hair of deceased family members—a common 19th century remembrance.

Many pieces throughout this house are of special interest to lovers of antique furniture. Of note in the master bedroom is the tall Kentucky cabinet (a c. 1830 armoire fitted with pegs for hanging clothes) In a child's bedroom there is a rare Midwestern corner chair. In another room is a musical instrument called a melodia (c. 1856-58), a piano-like instrument with folding legs so that it could be carried to church and social events. There is also a hoop chair (c. 1850-60), designed for ladies wearing hoop skirts, and a Kentucky bed and dresser (c. 1840). Allegedly, a Kentucky bridegroom carved the bed posts with his pocketknife!

Marshal's House at the Jail

The Marshal's dining room is now the museum gift shop. The kitchen—an outdoor summer kitchen to diminish the risk of fire and odors—was where the Marshal's wife cooked for her family and (for a fee) for prisoners.

This house was without certain amenities—such as closets and bathrooms—considered musts today. None-the-less, it was considered a fine residence in its day, and remains a handsome structure and a strong tie to regional history.

The jail next door has even stronger ties, since it housed the infamous and very popular Frank James—in style! Friends furnished his cell with furniture, rugs, and pictures—all the comforts of home, except a dining room. This he did not need, since he dined with the Marshal and his family in the Federal building right next door! That room, decorated as it might have been in those early days, welcomes visitors today to a very law-ful visit at the Marshal's historic house.

4 The piano in the Marshall House parlor was previously owned by a woman who was imprisoned for her Southern sympathies.

5 The Marsha l's 1850s pigeon-hole desk is an early forerunner of the home office.

Adams House

13

Deadwood, South Dakota

At the Adams House in Deadwood, South Dakota, Christmas candlelight falls softly on a Tiffany-style lamp, a settee gilded in gleaming gold leaf, and carefully polished woodwork. Hand-painted canvas walls, ornate plaster friezes, and stained glass create a luxurious background for upholstery and other textiles reproduced from original documents. In other rooms, chandeliers with Edison bulbs add warm light to rooms designed to enchant. This grand mansion, now beautifully restored, today stands as a testament to the tenacity and vision of the pioneers who made their fortunes in the fabled gold rush town where western legend Wild Bill Hickok was murdered. The history of the Adams House, like so many of America's other grand homes, is one of rags to riches, joy and sorrow.

The story of the home began when Harris and Anna Franklin decided to build a home reflective of their wealthy standing in the former rough and tumble mining camp. These immigrants of Jewish descent had won and lost and won again their fortune. When construction on the first architect-designed home built in Deadwood started in 1892, the Queen Anne style mansion was described as "the grandest house west of the Mississippi." The Franklins took great pride in the home they built and entertained frequently. Following Anna Franklin's death 1902, only child Nathan and wife Ada moved into the home which was sold to them three years later by their father for one dollar.

Like their parents, Nathan and Ada figured prominently as part of Deadwood's social elite. The local newspapers regularly reported on the elegant parties that they hosted and when they did something out of the ordinary, such as buying Deadwood's first modern automobile in 1905. Nathan Franklin was elected mayor in 1914 and served two terms. By 1920, he and Ada moved to New York City, selling the

When it was constructed in 1892, The Historic Adams House, a Queen Anne-style mansion in Deadwood, South Dakota, was called the grandest house west of the Mississippi. *Photographs courtesy the Historic Adams House, Deadwood, SD*

1

2

home at 22 Van Buren Street for $8,500 to pioneer businessman William Emery Adams and his wife Alice.

W.E. Adams moved to the Black Hills in 1877. Instead of panning for gold, he decided to sell pots and pans to those who did. He and his brother opened a grocery store which burned to the ground in 1879. Undaunted, Adams rebuilt, and by 1894, moved the business to Sherman Street. The progressive Mr. Adams' four-story building had a modern elevator powered by water. By 1901, Adams decided to concentrate on his wholesale business. It grew it into one of the largest businesses in the state.

Ironically, W.E. Adams bought the home from his political rival Nathan Franklin who beat Adams in the 1916 mayoral campaign. Adams who had already served four terms as mayor would later serve an additional two terms after purchasing the Adams House.

Despite Adams' business and political successes, he faced much sorrow in his personal life. Both of the Adams' daughters, Lucile and Helen, died as young adults. Lucile died of typhoid in 1912, and a grief-stricken Helen died in childbirth after learning of her mother Alice's death on June 6, 1925. Helen was buried holding her baby which died hours after delivery. In less than 48 hours, Adams had lost his entire family.

1 A beautifully-decorated Christmas Tree (a German custom that spread to the United States) is the focal point of an elaborately decorated foyer. Of special note is the deep frieze embellished with delicate floral swags that adds interest at ceiling height.

2 Throughout, the Adams House interiors boast richly milled woodwork such as that seen on the foyer fireplace with its fancy mirrored overmantel that reflects rich velvet draperies.

This grand mansion, now beautifully restored, today stands as a testament to the tenacity and vision of the pioneers who made their fortunes in the fabled gold rush town where western legend Wild Bill Hickok was murdered.

After so much sorrow, the Adams House was to know joy again. In 1927, at age 73, Adams married a 29-year-old widow, Mary Mastrovich Vicich. The difference in their ages, economic backgrounds, and the fact that he was Episcopalian and she Roman Catholic, created a scandal. Still, the couple lived happily together for seven years until Mr. Adams suffered a stroke and died in his home in June, 1934.

Mary Adams closed the house after the death of her husband and chose to only visit it with friends and admirers. Historic Adams House director Mary Kopco says, "Mary Adams told people that the house was haunted. Whether she truly believed that is unclear but her ghostly warning apparently protected the home from major vandalism and theft for over fifty years!"

The City of Deadwood bought the Adams House in 1992. Under the leadership of then Historic Preservation Officer Mark Wolfe and later Mary Kopco, the Adams House was returned to its original splendor. According to Kopco, "Some of the leading historic preservation experts in the United States undertook the Adams House restoration project. They accumulated extensive photographic and written documentation during the process, from the exterior work on the roof and foundation to the interior work of cleaning hand-painted canvas wall coverings and replicating wallpaper from the 1930s. The result is a fine example of the best that historic preservation can achieve."

The Adams House opened as a museum on July 1, 2000, to a joyful public that celebrates joyful Christmas seasons in this history-filled house.

Opposite: Hand-painted canvas walls, ornate friezes with delicate Adamesque swags, Tiffany lamps and chandeliers illuminated with original Edison bulbs, and hand-modeled tiles as fireplace surrounds add luxurious touches to the Adams House.

Adams House

Morris Butler House

14

Indianapolis, Indiana

A storytelling hour and Victorian tea are highlights of the "Victorians at home" holiday season at the elegant Second Empire style Morris-Butler House built in 1865, in the once-fashionable Old Northside neighborhood in Indianapolis.

A tour of the three-story house shows the fascinating architectural details and the decorative and domestic arts so dear to the hearts of home-loving Victorians.

In the formal parlor, rich warmly-colored walls are the perfect contrast to ornate crown molding painted a crisp classic white. In the corner sets a piano, ready for the musical concert, a favorite after-dinner form of entertainment.

In the High Victorian style, rooms feature decoratively stenciled ceilings, elaborately colored and dramatically scaled and patterned wallpapers, and ornate plasterwork.

Throughout the house, carefully restored interiors are filled with rare furnishings such as an ingenious Wooton desk, fine paintings, and sculpture.

The Morris-Butler House is named for two distinguished families who lived there at various times.

The Second Empire-style of the three-story Morris Butler House, an 1865 landmark in Indianapolis, features a characteristic dramatic central tower. *Photographs courtesy Historic Landmarks Foundation of Indiana/Morris-Butler House Museum*

In the High Victorian style, rooms feature decoratively stenciled ceilings, elaborately colored and dramatically scaled and patterned wallpapers, and ornate plasterwork

1 The bold red carpet, gilded frames, and ornate ceiling treatment create a stunning entry. *Photograph by Garry Chilluffo, Chilluffo Media; courtesy Historic Landmarks Foundation of Indiana/Morris-Butler House Museum*

2 The luxurious parlor and its brightly decorated Christmas tree greet holiday visitors. The oil portrait is part of a large permanent collection of 19th century art. *Photograph by Garry Chilluffo, Chilluffo Media; courtesy Historic Landmarks Foundation of Indiana/Morris-Butler House Museum*

Morris Butler House

The Morris Family

In 1864, John Morris, the son of an Indianapolis settler, commissioned the construction of the house on land he bought from Ovid Butler, founder of Butler University. The Morris family moved into their new home in 1865. Among the first to move to the new suburb now known as the Old Northside, they were soon joined by others who made the area the fashionable address in Indianapolis. They lived there until 1878.

The Butler Family

Noble Butler, a renowned bankruptcy lawyer, moved into the house three years later with his wife and seven young children. Members of the Butler family lived in the house until 1957, when Noble's youngest daughter, Florence, died. Over the years, the Old Northside had become home to low-income renters. Most of the buildings—including the once-stately Morris-Butler House—suffered from neglect, so heirs took what they

2

3

4

wanted from the house and auctioned the house and its contents. Museum records show that the house served as an art gallery before the Historic Landmarks Foundation of Indiana bought the house in 1964. Eli Lilly provided funds for restoring the house and in 1969 the splendid house was opened as the Morris-Butler House museum and educational center.

What tine is it?

The Morris-Butler House is about more than static displays. Educational programs include such sessions as "Elegance Remembered: Etiquette for Today." The Victorians practically invented the art of dining—placing great emphasis on the right fork for the right food.

Choosing the wrong fork or spoon was a serious social gaffe. But have no fear, using the wrong piece of silverware (or failing to crook your finger in the socially-accepted manner) at a holiday tea at the Morris-Butler House will not get you removed from the Indianapolis Social Register. "Our Victorian Holiday Teas, held three Saturdays in December, offer a relaxing afternoon of delicious teas and tea fare, a hand-made craft to take home, and lots of laughter in lovely surroundings," says Shannon Borbely, Museum Administrator.

For serious old house buffs, the "How to Research Your Historic Home" workshop under the leadership of Suzanne Stanis of Historic Landmarks Foundation of Indiana is designed to guide research, keeping the process fun.

To be sure, The Morris-Butler House is a vital place year 'round, but never more so than during the Christmas holidays season, when the lavishly decorated house exemplifies home as haven for body and soul.

3 The stately dining room is a feast for holiday eyes. *Photograph by Garry Chilluffo, Chilluffo Media; courtesy Historic Landmarks Foundation of Indiana/Morris-Butler House Museum*

4 Behind the dazzling Christmas tree, painted trim accentuates a niche, creating a strong focal point in this Victorian setting. *Photograph courtesy Historic Landmarks Foundation of Indiana/Morris-Butler House Museum*

5 A ornately carved and decorated mirror reflects the warmth of candlelight. *Photograph by Garry Chilluffo, Chilluffo Media; courtesy Historic Landmarks Foundation of Indiana/Morris-Butler House Museum*

6 The window—in the grand Victorian manner—is hung with light-controlling draw draperies, lace privacy curtains, and decorative swag and jabot topped by an elaborate carved and gilded cornice. Overhead, the complex ceiling molding is decoratively painted. *Photograph courtesy Historic Landmarks Foundation of Indiana/Morris-Butler House Museum*

Petersen House

15

Tempe, Arizona

Glaedelig Jul! — Merry Christmas!

Niels Petersen, a dashing sailor with the Danish merchant marine, traded the high seas for the high desert. In 1871, he arrived in Tempe, Arizona, bringing along Danish Christmas customs. Ultimately, he attracted enough Danes to Arizona to give it one of the nation's largest Danish immigrant populations. Now, the Petersen House Museum joins forces with the Danish Immigrant Museum in Elkhorn Iowa to celebrate every Christmas Danish style. "*Alles velkommen* (Everyone's welcome)," says Museum Administrator Amy A. Douglass:

We offer special programs throughout the holidays that both entertain and educate. Danish holiday songs are very popular. Visitors who know Danish are invited to sing along with Linda Rising and Karl Rehmer.

One of the most intriguing events is a demonstration of the Danish art of papir klip—literally clipping or cutting decorative shapes out of paper. One memorable Christmas, Annette Andersen of Kimballton, Iowa, demonstrated this captivating art. These shapes make intriguing Christmas ornaments. Along with Victorian decorations, we hang some on the tree, and others on the walls," says Amy. "We also offer some papir klip ornaments (imported directly from Denmark) for sale during the event.

One year, we were inspired by the fairy tales of Hans Christian Andersen, a notable Dane," says Amy. "The Princess on the Pea, The Little Match Girl, The Steadfast Tin Soldier, and The Ugly Duckling were interpreted through short skits performed by actors from the East Valley Children's Theater. Another year, decorations interpreted J. Krohn's Peter's Christmas, the story of a young boy's Christmas in Denmark in the late 1800s— about the time when Niels Petersen immigrated to Arizona. The author lived in a village a few miles from Niels' Danish home.

Niels Petersen, a wealthy Salt River Valley rancher, commissioned architect James Creighton to design and build his 1892 home which blends Victorian Queen Anne and Craftsman styles. A plaque commemorates the historic status of the Petersen House. *Photographs courtesy Tempe Historical Museum/Petersen House Museum*

As for refreshments, "The English have their tea time; the Danes have their coffee time. So, Danish treats and coffee are served to all our guests on Advent Sundays," Amy states.

About the house

On arriving in the Tempe area, Petersen homesteaded on 160 acres south of town in the Salt River Valley. He transformed his desert land into a successful ranch, becoming a U.S. citizen in 1878, leading businessman (one time president of the Farmers and Merchants Bank), and community leader (serving as a member of the Territorial Legislature (1895-96)," says Amy. By 1912, Petersen owned more than 2000 acres. Sadly, his first wife and their infant son died. In 1892, Petersen's position in the community encouraged him to exchange his adobe home with what is now known as the Petersen House, built by Petersen for his second wife, Susanna.

"Architecturally, the Petersen House now is a fascinating blend of Victorian era Queen Anne and Craftsman bungalow styles," says Amy. "It reveals its 1890s origins as designed by James Creighton, a prominent architect in territorial Arizona. Also visible is the remodeling that took place in 1930,

Back-to-back fireplaces between back and front parlors are decorated with Danish papir klip (cut paper) ornaments.

which introduced the popular bungalow style." Multi gables, a key Queen Anne element, create a complex roof line. Porches, gables, balconies, and bay windows add dimensional interest to the façade. Inside, 12-foot high ceilings and decorative surface treatments (including gold-leaf picture railing and hand-stenciled wallpaper borders) add elegance. Stained glass windows shield interiors from the desert sun and provide light and color play.

"The Petersen House was placed on the National Register of Historic Places in 1977," says Amy. "It was donated to the city of Tempe in 1979. The Tempe Historical Society assumed responsibility for coordinating the exterior restoration which took place in 1982. In the late 1980s, the Tempe Historical Museum oversaw the interior restoration. In 1990, the Petersen House received the Arizona Governor's Award for Historic Preservation.

"Niels Petersen achieved much for himself, his family, and Arizona," says Amy. "His house stands—in its original spot—as a monument to his accomplishments." Annual Christmas events at Petersen House celebrate the man and his Danish origin.

The Christmas tree in the front parlor is decorated with papir klip ornaments depicting Hans Christian Andersen tales. Themes may change from year-to-year, but ornaments always include papir klip art.

"Architecturally, the Petersen House now is a fascinating blend of Victorian era Queen Anne and Craftsman bungalow styles,"

1-2 Corner swags and cornice decorations enliven the walls at the Petersen House.

3-5 Trees throughout the house are decorated with papir klip (cut paper) ornaments, continuing a Danish hand-craft art tradition.

3

4

5

Florence Griswold House

16

Old Lyme, Connecticut

The Griswold House in Old Lyme, Connecticut is more than a magnificent example of the mature Late Georgian style architecture. It holds the "tale of how a serendipitous meeting of a prominent painter and a kindhearted landlady started a new chapter in American art history," according to its curators. This house—which features significantly in the history of American Impressionism—now The Florence Griswold Museum, is transformed for Christmas much in the way it might have been during its days as an artist colony

The holidays magically recapture the spirit of the early 20th century with horse-drawn carriage rides with Santa, *Christmastime Tea*, *A Very Merry Teddy Tea* for children, musical events, crafts workshops and gallery talks on how the artists who lived here celebrated the holiday. A holiday visit offers the chance to view an outstanding art collection in the context in which it was created and experience a remarkable collection that includes fine art, sculpture, works on paper, artist's studio material, toys and dolls, ceramics, furniture, textiles, decorative arts and historic artifacts, and the Lyme Historical Society Archives.

The center of the celebration is *Miss Florence's Artist Tree*. The tree is decorated with over seventy-five artists' palettes. Four other lavishly decorated trees grace the house. For the year 2006, other trees' decorations (the *Fantasy Trees*) were inspired by the ancient elements of Earth, Air, Fire and Water.

1 The Late Georgian-style Florence Griswold house was home to painters of the Lyme Art Colony, birthplace of American Impressionism, begun in the summer of 1900, and lasting three decades. In 1910, the house was painted this shade of yellow with dark green shutters. *Photographs courtesy The Florence Griswold Museum*

2 The spacious center hall with its grasscloth walls served as an art gallery. Typical of the Colony era, crepe paper bells and streamers hang from the ceiling, vases hold arrangements of dried plants from the gardens, and springs of greenery acorn artworks.

3 The Christmas tree stands in the parlor, where it appears that an artist has been cutting out felt letters for decoration. Vintage Christmas cards from the Florence Griswold collection are displayed on every possible surface.

The annual Christmas scavenger hunt is popular with young visitors.

Once upon a time...

The story of how the house became the center of the American Impressionist movement began when Miss Florence Griswold, an unmarried woman of nearly fifty years of age, who had outlived her parents and siblings, found herself alone, without means, and inheritor of the family home and its debts. She did the practical and socially acceptable thing—she turned her home into a boarding house. In 1899, Henry Ward Ranger, a well-regarded New York painter, paid a visit to the grand home. He vowed to return with other artists the following summer.

Ranger, who had recently returned from studying art in Europe, yearned to found an artists colony much like the French Barbizon. For him, Old Lyme had all the ingredients to make it the perfect setting for an emerging

school of American painting called Tonalism, a style of rendering moody landscapes, many with twilight and dusk as favored moods to depict. Miss Florence Griswold house was blessed with all the necessary features, much like those found in the prominent art colonies of France and Holland. According to Griswold House experts, the elegant home offered "a stimulating environment. artistic camaraderie, inexpensive lodging, and picturesque scenery." It was also conveniently located between the cultural hubs of Boston and New York and easily accessible, making available to artists the lush countryside of Connecticut. The Griswold House quickly attracted a cadre of artists.

The arrival of Childe Hassam in 1903 changed the focus of the colony toward Impressionism, thus resulting in its new identity as the "American Giverny," a reference to Claude Monet's gardens in France. Other artists such as Matilda Browne, William Chadwick and Willard Metcalf would later transform the house into the Lyme Art Colony.

The Colony flourished for over three decades, thanks to the endless beauty of New England's countryside and Miss Florence's hospitality. Hassam said that Griswold House was the place for "high thinking and low living," according to museum art historians. Perhaps he meant by this that artists could forsake the formal dining room for meals on the side porch, where they dined without jackets and ties and with rolled up sleeves.

4-5 Unwrapped presents were placed at the base of the tree, which in homes on tight budgets were decorated with homemade and impromptu items, At the Florence Griswold house, this included wooden artists' palettes. Now a tradition, seventy or more palettes donated by artists decorate the perennially popular "Artists Tree!"

The house became a locus for some of the most noted names in American Impressionism to paint many important works of art that are today part of museum and private collections across the nation. According to art historians at the Griswold House, "the intrinsic linkage of artist to locale defines the work of the Lyme Art Colony painters." Colony members painted *en plein air* (in the open air) and captured scenes of farmhouses, clapboard churches, gardens, granite ledges, salt marshes, wooden trestle bridges and grazing cows. By capturing the local and specific in a highly personal manner, say Griswold's curators, "these painters created a sense of permanence and continuity in a rapidly changing America … commemorated aspects of rural life reminiscent of New England's origins and celebrated the essential spirit of place."

In the formal dining room, where Woodrow Wilson and his family dined with Miss Florence and the artists, are some of the nearly forty works of art on wooden wall panels and doors left by departing artists. Plant decorations are from the extensive restored gardens of Miss Florence, an avid gardener.

The Florence Griswold House is a National Historic Landmark. William Noyes, impressed by architect Samuel Belcher's design for Old Lyme's First Congregational Church, commissioned the architect in 1817 to create a late Georgian-Style mansion.

The Civil War and advent of steam powered ships spelled economic doom for the town, but the once prosperous Griswold family turned the home into a school. Once Miss Florence turned the home into a boardinghouse for artists, various artists residing there began a tradition of painting door panels and panels in the dining room with "classic Old Lyme scenes" as well as scenes from far-away places.

A visit to the Florence Griswold House is a treat for art lovers. It's also a mecca for those who admire "Yankee ingenuity"—uncommon good sense—the kind that led a woman to transform a handsome house into an artists' haven and a unique museum that encompasses 11 acres along the Lieutenant River. In addition to the Griswold House, visitors can see a new riverfront gallery, a restored artist studio (much like the one used by famed American Impressionist Childe Hassam), an education center and the restored gardens which inspired so many artists.

6 The bedroom of Miss Florence is shown as she would have used it—as a place to wrap presents and write cards. The "Happy Birthday" card commemorates her sixtieth Christmas-Day birth date. The candy jar holds old-fashioned ribbon candy.

7 Like the house, the rustic barn—typical of those included in landscapes by resident artists—sports a simple wreath of greens with a red bow.

The Leu House

17

Orlando, Florida

There are many tourist attractions in Orlando, but only one historic house museum—the gracious Leu House. "Set among fifty acres of beautiful gardens, it is an ideal place in which to enjoy 'Old Florida' atmosphere—especially during the Christmas holidays," says Robert Bowden, Director.

Christmas at the Leu House is a lively time. "Decorating the House for the holidays has become a favorite tradition," says Bowden. Volunteers spend countless hours and loan decorations for the 12 rooms, two porches, two staircases, and four Christmas trees. "Interior designers volunteer their design talents, Notable among those who have decorated the house for several years are Ron Mummert and Dick Laferriere of Ron's Miniature Shop & Museum, who create remarkable miniature objects and diorama for display. Hardly is one season over than they're at work on the next!" Of course, the "designer showcase" décor is only part of an exciting holiday season that includes numerous events, advertised well in advance, for early planning.

"Old Florida" is a phrase that conjures images of a style not found in today's glitzy high-rise condominiums and monumental McMansions. "The Leu House is an excellent example of Old Florida living. Originally, it was a two-story, five-

Leu House, Orlando's only historic house museum, embodies the history of "Old Florida." Originally a small farmhouse, it was greatly expanded by New Yorker Duncan Clarkston Pell, who bought it in 1902. Photograph by Tracy Micciche, courtesy Leu House Museum, Harry P. Leu Garden

1

2

3

1-4 In the living room, bright white for mantel, chimney breast and woodwork contrasts crisply with gaily colored walls in a house that was a getaway for well-to-do New York owners. Flowers on the tree and garlands were handcrafted from Leu Gardens materials. Photograph of stair by Tracy Micciche; other photographs by Robert Bowden; courtesy Leu House Museum, Harry P. Leu Gardens.

"Set among fifty acres of beautiful gardens, it is an ideal place in which to enjoy "Old Florida" atmosphere—especially during the Christmas holidays," says Robert Bowden, Director.

5

room farm house, built in 1888 by John Thomas Mizell whose parents had been deeded the property in 1885. In 1902, New Yorker Duncan Clarkston Pell purchased and combined the several parcels of land, added two wings that doubled the size of the farmhouse, and planted an orange grove. Pell and silent screen star, Helen Gardner, used the house as a weekend get-away," Bowden states.

The third owners were Joseph and Martha Woodward, from Alabama, for whom the house was a winter retreat. In 1906, the Woodwards also added to the house. When Mrs. Woodward died in 1928, the estate went into trust and was rented out. "In 1936, Harry P. Leu bought the house now known as Leu House and 40 acres for $40,000. Their renovations included adding electricity and central plumbing to the 3,000 square foot house," says Mr. Bowden.

Leu, an Orlando native who had honed his business skills there before working outside Florida, moved back to Orlando at his widowed mother's request. He returned to work for a company for which he had worked in his early years, bought stock, and in 1926 gained control of the company and changed it to Harry P. Leu,

5-7 In the dining room with its mahogany Empire Period table and sideboard C. 1820, the sideboard is decorated with miniatures created by Ron's Miniature Shop and Museum. Flowers on the Christmas tree were handcrafted from dried plant materials from the famed Leu Gardens. Photographs by Robert Bowden, courtesy Leu House Museum, Harry P. Leu Gardens.

Inc. He married Mary Jane Schmidli in 1932. The couple enjoyed traveling the world together and bringing back exotic plants for their garden. Leu's interest in the garden and his cultivation and development of plants caused some to call him Florida's "Johnny Appleseed."

Leu sold his business in 1940, but stayed on to head the business until the mid-50s when he retired. Afterwards, he was involved in civic and social affairs. Notably, he helped finance the Greater Orlando Chamber of Commerce. "His many accomplishments on behalf of his beloved Orlando

6

7

culminated in the Leus gifting the city with The Leu House and gardens in 1961," says Bowden.

The house was used for some time as office space for gardening personnel and as classroom space. "Happily, in 1975, the Opera Guild chose the Leu House as its Designer Showcase House. The Leu's were honorary co-chairman of the event," Bowden notes.

As with all designer showcases, noted area interior designers "make over" rooms with new treatments for walls, floors, and ceiling, window treatments, furniture and accessories. Leading designers whose work was showcased in the 1975 Showcase included Jeanette McKean, Sam Ewing, and Warren Arnett. The work of these and other talented designers called attention once again to the beauty of the Leu House.

"Three years later, the Orange County Historical Society proposed making the Leu House a historic house museum. Headed by Jean Yothers and Patty Edwards, the Historical Society signed a

8-9 In the study, decorated for the season by Ron's Miniature Shop and Museum, a faux Santa is seated at Harry P. Leu's desk. *Photographs by Robert Bowden, courtesy Leu House Museum, Harry P. Leu Gardens*

11

13

12

10-12 On a chest in the master bedroom is a framed picture of Mr. Pell's second wife, Helen Louise Gardner (1884-1968), a silent screen star. She was the first woman film star to form her own company (The Helen Gardner Picture Corporation, Tappan, New York, 1912-1914). The ornate walnut bed is from the Victorian Period, C.1860. *Photographs by Robert Bowden, courtesy Leu House Museum, Harry P. Leu Gardens; holiday interior design and decoration by Interior Design students of Seminole Community College*

13 Mrs. Mary Jane Leu's bedroom is furnished with her original Jenny Lind style spool bed (C. 1890), night stand (C. 1825), and Empire style dressing table with bench and mirror. The mirror is Chippendale/Queen Anne style, C.1830. *Photograph by Robert Bowden, courtesy Leu House Museum, Harry P. Leu Gardens; holiday interior design and decoration by Interior Design students, Seminole Community College*

13

lease and began restoration work on the first floor," Bowden recounts. "The Harry P. Leu Foundation donated $15,000 for the project," he says, "and the City of Orlando restored the structure. The aging roof was replaced. The sagging porch near the dining room was repaired. And, the house was treated for termites—a real threat to wooden structures in Florida's damp climate." Bowden notes that a new central entrance was added to the north side of the house, expanding views of the lake from inside the house. "The object of the renovation was not an exhaustive, exacting

15

16

restoration of the house at any one of its several stages of development, but to create a well-to-do Florida house typical of the turn of the century." That, of course, is what the Leu House is—a wonderful trip back in time to Old Florida—the only such house in Orlando!

13-16 Designers at Ron's Miniature Shop and Museum go all out to decorate the children's rooms for the holidays, filling them with decorations, toys galore, and tasty treats for Santa! *Photographs by Robert Bowden, courtesy Leu House Museum, Harry P. Leu Gardens*

The kitchen gets its fair share of fanciful decorations for the holidays, thanks to designers from Ron's Miniature Shop and Museum. *Photographs by Robert Bowden, courtesy Leu House Museum, Harry P. Leu Gardens*

Baldwin-Reynolds House

18

Meadville, Pennsylvania

Every Christmas is exciting at the handsome Baldwin-Reynolds House, which, over the years, has been home to a US Supreme Court justice and two Meadville mayors.

Visitors approaching the house are welcomed by the sight of decorated trees—some grace the two-story wrap-around verandah influenced by Southern Greek Revival architecture of the early 19th century.

Indoors, bi-annually, guests thrill to the *Trees of Christmas* celebration presented by the Meadville Garden Club. Rooms throughout the twenty-five room house boast a uniquely decorated live Christmas tree. Guests enjoy the evening "tour of trees" and a program that includes live music by accomplished musicians. An accompanying "Christmas Boutique" offers unusual handmade items priced for any budget. Once, fever-pitch excitement occurred at the "Tree Auction," when aggressive bidders vied for a beautifully decorated "Baldwin-Reynolds Trees of Christmas" evergreen. Alas, that is no longer a tradition. One can only hope that it will be revived.

Each Christmas season, events keep Baldwin-Reynolds House alive as memory-maker as well as lovingly maintained repository of memories of times past. And what memories these walls hold! Following are Curator Joshua F. Sherretts' highlights, beginning with a brief account of the life of founder Henry Baldwin.

The 1843 Baldwin-Reynolds Greek Revival house in northwestern Pennsylvania—based on a Tennessee house called Hunter Hill and described as "the Mount Vernon of Meadville"—was built by Supreme Court Justice Henry Baldwin. *All photographs courtesy Baldwin-Reynolds House Museum*

Holiday celebrations in this house are reminders of the investment of themselves and their resources made by former residents.

Brief History of a Fine Old House

Before coming to Meadville as a deputy attorney general (now called district attorney), Henry Baldwin began practicing law in the first years of the 19th century under Alexander Dallas in Philadelphia. He served in this role for several years before moving to Pittsburgh to try his hand in iron foundries. Eventually he became a member of the United States House of Representatives, representing the 14th District. Baldwin quickly rose to national prominence as one of the few representatives who would defend Andrew Jackson's invasion of Florida during the First Seminole War in 1818. He became a rather famous national politician and a major player in Jackson's winning the 1828 presidential election in Pennsylvania.

Baldwin hoped for the Secretary of the Treasury position, but found himself passed over for this job. When Supreme Court Justice Bushrod Washington died in 1829, Jackson appointed Henry Baldwin to fill the position. Confirmed in two days, Baldwin remained on the bench until his death.

"Mount Hope" and the Baldwin House. *As Henry Baldwin aged, he and his wife Sarah ("Sally" Ellicott) Baldwin decided to settle down in Meadville (the place of Henry's early career), closer to friends and Sally's siblings when the Supreme Court was not in session.*

The 64-year-old Baldwin, while visiting his son in Tennessee, fell in love with a house there known as "Hunter Hill," and drew plans to this house to bring with him back to Meadville. In 1842, he and his wife settled on a 24 ½ acre estate on Terrace Street, property previously owned by Revolutionary War veteran, Samuel Lord, who affectionately called his home "Mount Hope." (The name lives on as the street name for the road near the rear of the house.) Lord lost the property to a sheriff sale in 1838, and Sally's sister's family bought and owned the lot until the Baldwin's arrival in 1842

The Baldwins began building their dream home in 1842, and by late summer 1843, were able to move into the unfinished house. Baldwin suddenly died while closing up his law office in Philadelphia on April 21, 1844. Because he had almost no money, friends paid for a modest funeral and Baldwin was buried in Oak Hill Cemetery in Washington, D.C. The Supreme Court Justice had not lived in his home a year.

The Baldwin Institute. Upon her husband's death, Sally Baldwin leased the property to the Meadville Female Seminary. Within three years, The Baldwin Institute was in search for a smaller building in Meadville. The estate was turned back over to Baldwin's widow in 1847.

"Mr. Meadville" moves in*. Sally Baldwin deeded the original 24 ½ acres along with an additional 38 acres she purchased that year to her nephew, William Reynolds. Reynolds, a graduate of Allegheny College and a Pittsburgh attorney, moved his wife Julia and one year old daughter Frances to Meadville that year (1847).*

Reynolds became a pillar in the community, serving as one of the most influential businessmen in town. One time President of the Meadville Gas and Water Company, his was the first house in Meadville to receive natural gas lighting. Reynolds, one of its founders, served as the first President of the Atlantic and Great Western Railroad. The last burgess of Meadville, he was the city's first mayor.

William and Julia spent many of their early years in the house remodeling the southern style plantation into their dream Victorian home. Pine woodwork was removed and replaced with black walnut, parquet floors were added over the existing pine, and new fireplaces, a library, and solarium were added. The most extensive renovation was the addition of a full third floor for both childrens' bedrooms and servants' quarters. William and Julia, revered members of the community, had four children. After living in their home for 60 years, the couple passed away in early 1911, one week apart.

A New Generation Moves In*. William and Julia Reynolds left their home and most of its contents to John Earle Reynolds, youngest of their four children. A few months later, in May 1911, John (a bachelor in his early 50s) married his longtime love, Katherine Shryock. The couple took a year-long honeymoon to Europe and Asia, evidenced by the 1912 Belgian wallpaper in the dining room, as well as other artifacts throughout the house. John Earle was a three term mayor of Meadville, as well as the President and Chairman of Merchant's Bank of Meadville. Katherine, active in the American Red Cross, was a charter member of the Meadville Garden Club. John and Katherine were the ideal socialites in Meadville and examples of true elegance.*

—Joshua F. Sherretts, Curator

Baldwin-Reynolds House

After John's death in 1947, Katherine remained in the house until her death in 1963, willing a public sale, Josh notes. The Crawford County Historical Society purchased the property and has kept it as a house museum, getting much of the Baldwin and Reynolds family furnishings back, as well as displaying items from the people of Crawford County. Holiday celebrations in this house are reminders of the investment of themselves and their resources made by former residents. In a sense, the Baldwin-Reynolds House is their gift that keeps on giving.

1-2 Vintage ornaments decorate Christmas trees throughout the 25-room house known for its annual *Trees of Christmas* celebration presented by the Meadville Garden Club.

3 A Christmas Card announced the *Trees of Christmas*, 2006 exhibition.

Entertaining Baldwin-Reynolds Style

Katherine Reynolds was recognized as an accomplished hostess, who planned every occasion to perfection. For ten years after the death of her husband, she continued her role as consummate hostess, preparing her home for holiday guests. Food from her kitchen was considered the finest in town. Curator Joshua Sherretts notes her Christmas1959 menu.

Christmas Day 1959

Cocktails
Goutees
Salted Nuts

Consumme Soup
Town House Crackers
Celery
Large Olives

Roast Turkey with Stuffing
Whipped Potatoes
Gravy

Cranberry Sauce
Chestnuts
Creamed Onions
String Beans
Orange and Grapefruit Salad

Candy Sticks

Plum Pudding
Golden Sauce

After Dinner Coffee
Candy

Joel Lane House

19

Raleigh, North Carolina

What a delightful idea: Awaken during the Christmas holidays in Wake County, North Carolina. Enjoy holiday festivities at the Joel Lane House, home of the man known as both the Father of Wake County and Father of Raleigh.

In the beginning (circa 1770), in the back country of North Carolina—before there was a Wake County—the house of planter Joel Lane stood. In 1771, Lane introduced the bill calling for the creation of Wake County in honor of Margaret Wake, wife of colonial Governor William Tryon. Some 20 years later (1792), Lane sold 1000 acres of his land to the new state of North Carolina for the creation of a permanent capital city, Raleigh. To preserve this scene of a great deal of North Carolina's and American history, the National Society of Colonial Dames of America purchased the house. It was moved from its original site circa 1910-1914, a short distance (about 100 yds.) to its current site.

Lane, who owned several thousand acres of land in the county, built his story-and-a-half house at a county crossroads—in the wilderness. Modest by today's standards, the Lane house was considered grand in its day. And to be sure, grand things happened there.

Today, the Joel Lane house—in what became a perennially popular style—seems so familiar and its setting so urban, most Americans will feel entirely at home. Especially at Christmas, when all are welcome! Then, the house—which had been lived in from the time of its construction until shortly before it was purchased by the Colonial Dames—is decorated with care and abuzz with the activities of the dearest of familial holidays.

"Christmas events at the Joel Lane House continue a 30-year tradition," says Curator Isabella P. Long. "On Saturday and Sunday afternoons of the first weekend in December, the public is invited to come and enjoy activities that would have occurred during gatherings in North Carolina from the early Colonial Period through early 19th century. Artifacts vital to life in colonial times are on display (and cannot be handled), but visitors may handle replicas and guess their uses!

Entrances to the charmingly unpretentious Joel Lane hint little of the extraordinary history of the house and its fascinating interior.

1

2

3

4

5

6

Holiday decorations true to those early days underscore the Period ambience. "Since our property dates from around 1770, we keep decorations as simple as possible," says Isabella.

Guests are treated to musical performances. In 2008, the Triangle Mountain Dulcimers played Christmas carols on Saturday afternoon. Pianist Wynne Coleman performed on Sunday afternoon. Her lively music added to the upbeat ambience, Isabella recalls, "I played approximately fifty or more short compositions ranging chronologically from the middle Baroque period to the early Classical period," says Wynne.

"Compositions included dances of the period such as Minuets, Gavottes Gigues, Sarabandes and Hornpipes. I also played a few Marches (such as 'King William's March' by an English composer, Jeremiah Clarke, who lived from 1659-1707). And, I added some simple basic musical forms such as Preludes, Fughettas, Rondos, and Theme and Variations."

1 In the kitchen, a traditional pineapple-and-greens centerpiece is prepared for the dining room table.

2 A pomegranate tree near the rear door shows its beautiful colored fruit.

3-4 Boldly-painted floorcloths add pattern to the passageway floor and terminate at a staircase with a newel post topped with greenery.

5 A glimpse of the dining room can be seen beyond a decorated newel post. Chippendale chairs and a round table set before the brick-lined fireplace with its arched opening and painted-panel chimney breast.

6 Fruit filled blue-and-white and filigree porcelain bowls create beautiful, edible decorations.

Modest by today's standards, the Lane house was considered grand in its day. And to be sure, grand things happened there.

7

7 In the parlor, a tea table sets before the fireplace, which is similar in design to that in the dining room, but here, the paneled chimney breast is of dark wood. Prized articles in this room include a Bible box and a Chippendale mirror.

8 Pewter candlesticks, old books and letters, and seasonal greenery decorate a desktop.

8

9

10

11

12

9 Seasonal greens crown the upstairs landing newel post.

10–11 A candle and greens on the windowsill add a holiday touch to the Lane's simply furnished bedroom.

12 The view from the window of the upstairs landing.

13

14

15

16

15 A beautiful toile fabric brightens the small parlor bedroom, creating a sense of coziness.

16 An antique hatbox makes an interesting bedroom accessory.

17

18

"Costumed re-enacters add an air of authenticity each Christmas. Costumed docents chat with guests. They provide invaluable information about the house, former occupants, period customs, historical events and more," notes Isabella. "Another annual custom—the bake sale—always provides guests the opportunity to take home tasty treats, reminders of holiday time well spent. And we're happy to share the Joel Lane House Christmas Cookie recipe."

17-20 From every angle, the kitchen is a fascinating study in architecture, door hardware, furniture (including the unique ladderback chair and red-painted storage cupboard), and kitchen tools and equipment (including the large churn for making butter).

21

21 Old timbers acd textural interest and warmth to the kitchen.

22 Wreaths on the rusty-red painted kitchen door acknowledge the season.

23 Costumed re-enacters man food tables with their baskets of baked goodies, and the popular wassail bowl at the holiday Bake Sale.

In 1792, the legislature bought 1,000 acres of Lane land on which to establish city of Raleigh, to be the center of state government and the permanent state capital.

24

Brief history

When Lane (c. 1740-1795) built the house, the area was a crossroads hamlet of colonial Johnston County. "His house stood on a small hill near the main trail through the area which was sparsely settled," says Kathy Ruse, Assistant Curator. Lane was a socially conscious and politically active man who accomplished much. She says: "In 1770, Lane, as a member of the colonial General Assembly, successfully worked to create Wake County. A year later, Wake's first county court convened at his home. Shortly after, a courthouse and other buildings were constructed, and the hamlet near the home became known as "Wake Court House." Lane was made a member of the court, a lifetime position. In 1782, Lane served in the state Senate and attended the majority of sessions from 1782 until 1794. "He was a delegate to the 1789 convention in Halifax which ratified

25

26

the U.S. Constitution," Kathy says. In 1792, the legislature bought 1,000 acres of Lane land on which to establish city of Raleigh, to be the center of state government and the permanent state capital.

Because the Joel Lane house looks so familiar, it would be easy to simply drive by. To fail to visit, is to miss a trip back to the beginnings of the United States of America. Best to plan to stop awhile, and reflect on the life of Joel Lane and his many contributions to state and national history. "Enjoy traditional refreshments (including the regionally famous Joel Lane Christmas Sugar Cookies), and bask in the blessings of the season—blessings we enjoy because of Joel Lane.

24-26 Costumed re-enacters man food tables with their baskets of baked goodies, and the popular wassail bowl at the holiday Bake Sale.

Cookie-making is an art and an annual event at the Joel Lane House. *Photographs by Kathleen C. Ruse, courtesy Joel Lane Museum House*

JOEL LANE CHRISTMAS SUGAR COOKIES 2008

2 cup butter
1-1/2 cup 10xx sugar
1 egg
1 teaspoon vanilla
1/2 teaspoon almond extract
2-1/2 cup flour
1 teaspoon baking soda
1 teaspoon cream of tartar

Mix thoroughly butter, confectioners' sugar, egg, vanilla and almond extract. Blend in flour, soda and cream of tartar. Cover and chill 2 to 3 hours.

Heat oven to 375 degrees
Divide dough in half
Roll to ¼" thickness on lightly floured surface
Cut into desired shapes
Place on lightly greased cookie sheet
Bake 7 to 8 minutes or until light brown on edge
Makes about 2 doz. cookies, depending on shapes

Recipe provided by The Joel Lane House

Royal Icing

This smooth, hard drying icing makes decorations that last for months without softening, if stored properly. Royal icing decorations should be air dried. Allow several hours drying time for large decorations. Make sure bowl and utensils are grease free, since any trace of grease will cause royal icing to break down. Royal icing dries quickly, so keep icing bowl covered with a damp cloth at all times. Store in an air tight container. Rebeat at low speed before using. Thin out with water to make it spreadable. For piping bags leave stiff.

NOTE: *Royal icing is edible. Since it dries candy-hard, it is not recommended for icing cakes. Use only for special effects that you want to last.*

ROYAL MERINGUE RECIPE

3 level tablespoons Wilton Meringue Powder Mix

4 cups sifted confectioners sugar

6 tablespoons water

Add a little extract of choice. Almond is good.

NOTE: When using large counter top mixer or for stiffer icing, use 1 tablespoon less water. Beat all ingredients at low speed for 7 to 10 minutes (10 to 12 at high speed for portable mixer) until icing forms peaks. Yield: 3 cups

Additional decorations include Sparkling Sugars, Confetti, Christmas Jimmies, and Twinkling Trees mix.

Recipe provided by The Joel Lane House

Crocker House Museum

20

Mount Clemens, Michigan

One of the most exciting places to celebrate Christmas in charming Mount Clemens, Michigan is the handsome Crocker House at 15 Union Street. A house museum, it is one of the more important cultural attractions in this 4 1/2-square mile city devoted to quality of life.

Lively and welcoming, the Crocker House is connected to a local political dynasty of sorts. In 1869, Joshua Dickinson, the first mayor of Mount Clemens (and grandson of the town's founder, Christian Clemens), built the dignified residence in another location. In 1870, his daughter, Katherine married George M. Crocker and they moved into the house. At Joshua Dickinson's death, Crocker, a former prosecuting attorney and justice of the peace, became mayor. Their home became a center of social activity.

Carolers sing on the porch of the Crocker House. Built in 1869 by Joshua Dickinson, the Italianate-style structure became the Crocker House when his Dickinson's daughter Katherine moved into the house with her husband, George Crocker, in 1870. *Photographs by Marcia Swiderski, courtesy Crocker House Museum*

1-2 At Christmas time, visitors gather around the decorated tree and pump organ in the cozy parlor for Christmas sing-along sessions.

3 Antique wallpaper is a charming backdrop for a display of tasty tidbits.

Crocker House Museum

In 1908, the house was moved to make room for a new post office. The Crocker family continued to make this house their home, and owned it until 1921. Then, Max Cohen purchased the home, remodeled it into four apartments, and lived there until his new residence was built in 1927. In 1934, Harry Chevalier purchased the home and resided there until the 1970s. At that point the Michigan State Highway Department purchased the home for $17,000. In 1975, it was slated for removal or demolition. In stepped the Macomb County Historical Society, which rescued the house. In 1976, this group moved the Crocker House to Union Street for use as a local-history museum

Now a museum, Crocker House is devoted to the history of Mount Clemens. "Walking through its rooms is like walking back into the late 1800s, when Mount Clemens was known as a great resort. People from around the world came to this bucolic town to enjoy its famous mineral baths," says Director Kimberly Parr.

During that late Victorian era, Christmas was perhaps the most important family holiday. Under Ms. Parr's direction, Crocker House is abuzz year 'round with activities for the whole family, but in the fall, a crescendo begins that culminates in Christmas holiday events. Ms. Parr says:

Clove-studded oranges bob in the wassail bowl—part of the "Victorian Christmas Wallow & Wassail" event, a Christmas tradition at the Crocker House.

On December 6, parents accompany their children to the very popular St. Nickolas Day Celebration. That's the day that Europeans celebrate St. Nickolas Day. In Europe, children leave their shoes by the door so that St. Nick can fill them with treats. We encourage children who are guests that day to leave their shoes in the hallway. St. Nick will arrive, greet them, and pose for photographs with them in the parlor!

A highlight is the luncheon—replete with story-telling and caroling, accompanied by someone (perhaps Barbara Parr, Kimberly's mother) at the pump organ. A "make and take" craft session rounds out a full day of fun. Children who have been enrolled in earlier Crocker House Etiquette sessions will have an opportunity to show off their newly-acquired manners!

Adults look forward to the Victorian Christmas event which includes favorite holiday activities. In the parlor, there is Christmas caroling accompanied by the pump organ. In the kitchen, there is a candy-making demonstration. Refreshments—very important to Victorians—are sumptuous. We serve a full Afternoon Tea. There is hot 'Three Wives Tea,' sconces with Devonshire cream and jam, and a variety of tea sandwiches. Oh yes—and dessert!

The Victorian Christmas Wallow & Wassail appeals to adults and children. Carolers meander through the house and grounds, providing a musical background. Guests may sip hot wassail, taste a hearty Brunswick stew served in a bread-bowl, and enjoy Christmas cookies. In the kitchen, there's sugar plum and marzipan candy-making demonstrations. Children may make take-home crafts. And of course, everyone may greet St. Nicholas, who never misses this event!

Lively and welcoming, the Crocker House is connected to a local political dynasty of sorts.

4

5

6

4-5 Candy-making demonstrations are a big hit during the Christmas season. Marzipan in amusing figurative shapes is a favorite.

6 Roasting chestnuts fill the air with the aroma of Christmas.

7 The charming gazebo silhouetted against a fire-red setting sun marks the beginning of evening holiday festivities at the Crocker House.

7

Calvin B. Taylor House

21

Berlin, Maryland

Museums are magicians—conjuring the past, relating it to the present, and preserving its meanings for the future. That's what the house at 208 North Main Street in Berlin, Maryland does–energetically each season and especially at Christmas time. Then, the rooms are decorated with fresh evergreens, the mouth-watering fragrance of gingerbread fills the air, and a full wassail bowl greets guests. The highlight of the season which begins in late November and continues through December, is the Classical Christmas Dinner and Concert which features a gourmet dinner in the historic Atlantic Hotel's dining room, followed by a concert in the historic house museum.

Very popular during the holidays are the horse-drawn carriage rides throughout Berlin's Historic District. And while a ride in a horse-drawn carriage down the bucolic streets of Berlin, Maryland is fun, it fuels no images of daring deeds by past citizens. Who on a bright, sunny Christmas Day could possibly conjure the dark night of February 16, 1804, when Lieutenant Stephan Decatur (who was born in Berlin) took the U.S. Navy ship *Intrepid* into Tripoli harbor to destroy the captured U.S. frigate *Philadelphia?* British Admiral Lord Nelson reportedly called it "the most bold and daring act of the Age." Lieutenant Decatur became an instant national hero. Subsequent deering-do made him the youngest-ever naval Captain and later a Commodore.

Who could recall scenes in *Planet of The Apes*, which made Linda Harrison a Hollywood star, then conjure images of her strolling along as a Berlin youngster the same narrow streets that the carriage is navigating?

1-2 Throughout December—whether or not Christmas is white (with snow)—carriage rides pass the 1832 Federal style Calvin B. Taylor home, a symbol of Berlin, Maryland's historic past. *Photographs courtesy Calvin B. Taylor House Museum*

3 The fanlight, sidelights, and green-painted panel door decorated with a colorful wreath create a graceful entry, outside and in.

Less well-known than Decatur or Harrison, but perhaps more important to the city of Berlin was teacher, lawyer, and founder of his eponymous bank, Calvin B. Taylor. It is his dignified Federal style house at 208 North Main Street, that is now a museum dedicated to bringing to life the inspiring history of Berlin and its many colorful citizens.

Museum spokesperson Susan Taylor says:

> *The Calvin B. Taylor House Museum presents Berlin's history through exhibits depicting life from the early 1800s to the present day. Local antiques, artifacts and transcribed oral histories allow visitors a glimpse into the lives of many who left a mark on local history and modern culture. Calvin B. Taylor was one such citizen. The bank he founded in 1890, is still in operation today.*

And so is his house!

The fanlight, sidelights, and carved panel door are luxury notes at the entry.

Calvin B. Taylor House

A brief history

The house at 208 North Main Street is a classic Federal style residence built in 1832 by Isaac Covington, whose family lived there during the Civil War. A later occupant, local businessman and farmer Robert J. Henry, who helped bring the railroad to Berlin, used the house as a townhouse. The house is named for its most famous occupant, Calvin B. Taylor, who lived there from the 1890s until his death in 1932, after which the house suffered a decline in fortune. It was about to be demolished and the grounds made into a parking lot when citizens

In the dining room, Federal style architecture and furnishings are in harmony with the style of the house.

Museums are magicians—conjuring the past, relating it to the present, and preserving its meanings for the future.

4-6 In the parlor, a portrait of Mary White, a noted Berlin citizen, hangs over the fireplace mantel. The 19th century sofa was made in Philadelphia, a noted furniture center of the era. The drop leaf table gains an arrangement of greenery and berries during the holidays.

5

6

formed The Berlin Heritage Foundation in 1981. They persuaded the city to buy it in 1982, and allow the Foundation to administer the house as a museum. The city paid $30,000 for the house, and the Foundation raised $100,000 to restore it and open the Calvin B. Taylor House Museum on October 2, 1983.

Interesting architectural details

The house is interesting to architects who study the front doorway's engaged fluted columns and butterfly modillions—design elements repeated on the living room mantel. Hand-restored graining on the interior doors by noted grainers Linda Croxson and Philip Ward lends an authentic note to doors and paneling. Stained glass windows and the west wing, added by the Taylors, attest to their affluence. Today, the Harrison Room in the west wing, is dedicated to the history of the Harrison family's successful Berlin nursery business.

Furnishings of interest

Furnishings of note include a 19th century sofa made in Philadelphia, an 1825 Eagle pattern quilt, a corner cupboard that belonged to the Betsy Ross family, fine Sheffield silver candlesticks, blue-and-white Staffordshire transfer china, and an oil portrait of Mary White, whose husband built their historic 1810 "Robin's Nest" house, which still exists at West and Broad Streets in Berlin, Maryland.

Perhaps the most visited space is the Man o' War exhibit, chockful of memorabilia relating to the great racehorse, sire of War Admiral and grandsire of Seabiscuit. After visiting that room, it's only natural to consider a horse-drawn carriage ride—a jolly end to a merry Maryland Christmas.

7 The most-visited space is the Man O' War exhibit, with copious memorabilia relating to the great sire of War Admiral and grandsire of Seabiscuit.

8 Trees grace areas throughout the house, including this hallway with its eye-catching black-and-white diamond patterned floor.

9 In the second floor hallway stands a prized plantation desk.

10 Not all rooms are decorated to the teeth in the Victorian style—something visitors accustomed to that more-is-better-and-essential mode find restraint startling!

7

8

9

10

The Pettingill-Morron House

22

Peoria, Illinois

What's playing in Peoria at Christmas time? What a silly question. Peoria's list of "things to do during the Holidays" leaves even the most energetic breathless. There's the Annual Santa Parade in Downtown Peoria, America's longest running holiday parade—replete with costumed characters, novelty units, floats, local marching bands and Santa Claus! "Yule Like Peoria" (love the catchy name) features holiday entertainment throughout the downtown, where businesses offer special displays and entertainment. The Luthy Botanical Gardens' Candlelight Walks delight. So does the East Peoria Festival of Lights. Executive director Amy L. Kelly says:

Best of all Christmas-in-Peoria happenings is the Candlelight tour of the elegant Pettengill-Morron House Museum, where costumed guides escort visitors through beautifully decorated rooms, regaling with tidbits of history made in these very rooms. There is always a Christmas theme at The Pettengill-Morron House. One year, it was All Through the House, with scents of baking cookies and fresh greenery permeating the air and sounds of Christmas carols wafting throughout.

In 1900, a colonial revival porch and porte cochere were added to the Pettingill-Morron house, which was built in 1868 in the Second Empire style. *Photographs by Amy Kelly, courtesy Pettingill-Morron House*

1

2

3

1 Philanthropist Jean Morron, who lived in the Pettingill-Morron house from 1953 to 1966, considered etiquette essential and held teas in her home that required much silver and fine china. Three generations of silver are displayed in the dining room.

2-3 In preparation for the annual candlelight tour, a hallway mirror and console are swagged with evergreen garlands, while in the library, a top hat and Morron's great-grandfather's 1763 college diploma—on real sheepskin—are displayed.

The Pettingill-Morrow House

The community gets involved, keeping the historic Pettengill-Morrow House a very lively part of Peoria's present. Kelly says, "The Peoria Garden Club assists with decorations for each of the eleven rooms in the Second Empire-style house built by Moses Pettengill in 1868. And one year, talented area designer David Rogers displayed antique dolls and toys.

In addition to the museum's permanent collection of unique objects from several Peoria families, there may be a special exhibit. Our *Silhouettes of Lincoln* exhibit was very popular, perhaps because he and the Pettingills were very good friends, and it's said that Lincoln visited the Pettingills. We plan and announce special exhibits well in advance, because the holiday season in Peoria is a busy time—and lovers of Christmas will want to stop by this house.

A Tiffany lamp, with its stained glass globe, augments candlelight for the romantic tour.

One year, it was All Through the House, with scents of baking cookies and fresh greenery permeating the air and sounds of Christmas carols wafting throughout.

Brief history

The Pettingill-Morron House preserves a part of Peoria's rich history," says Amy. "Briefly, the house was built in 1868 by Moses Pettengill and his wife, Lucy, natives of New Hampshire who came here in 1834. Moses had a successful hardware store and was a leader in the Presbyterian Church.

The couple were actively involved in the anti-slavery movement, becoming conductors on the Underground Railroad and housing freedom-seeking runaway slaves at their earlier home on Jefferson Street (torn down, to make way for a hotel). Lucy Pettengill lead the Female Anti-Slavery Society of Peoria in 1843, and later helped form the statewide Female Anti-Slavery Society of Illinois. They were close friends with Abraham Lincoln.

After the Pettingills' residency, four other families lived in the house (1892-1953). Amy says, "Two made changes to the original structure: the Clarks (1892-1901) installed wooden hall floors; the Stones (1945-1953) updated the bathrooms.

The bedroom with its handsome mahogany bed is included in the tour. Of particular interest is a sterling silver hair brush set said to have belonged to a Russian Czar, Alexandrovitch.

The kitchen, with the colorful, decorated corner cabinet, contains (out of sight here) a set of prized antique copper cookware.

But, the most significant changes were made by Jean Morron, who bought the house in 1953 and lived there until her death in 1966. "In a room that was her new library, Mrs. Morron installed a fireplace from her previous home and replaced carved wood paneling with wallpaper. She also installed new lighting. She also added the decorative iron fence that surrounds the lawn, and a three-car garage.

In 1967, the Pettengill-Morron House was opened to the public. In 1976, the home was listed in the National Register of Historic Places.

Collections

Most of the furnishings in the Pettingill-Morron House were left there by Mrs. Morron at her death in 1966, when the house and its contents were given to the Peoria Historical Society. "Of particular interest are a Tiffany lamp (that was discovered in a box with the label 'John's ugly lamp'), a sterling silver hairbrush set said to have belonged to Czar Nicholas Alexandrovith, Mrs. Morron's family silverware, and antique copper cookware. There are, of course, many other interesting pieces, including a fainting couch—a timely piece of furniture for most of us during the holiday season in Peoria," says Amy, with a laugh.

Slifer House

23

Lewisburg, Pennsylvania

Slifer House is unique—a museum on the campus of River Woods Senior Living Community. Owned and operated by Albright Care Services and staffed in part by residents of the Community, "Slifer House is decorated at Christmas time in Victorian finery for the viewing pleasure of the public," says Museum Director Gary Parks.

Slifer House, home of Eli Slifer, prominent in Pennsylvania politics, is a Tuscan-style mansion by Samuel Sloan, an eminent Philadelphia architect. It was built during the early days of the American Civil War. Today, it is part of the campus of River Woods Senior Living Community, owned by Albright Car Services. *Photographs by Heather Ervin, courtesy Slifer House Museum*

Gary describes Christmas 2008—typical in scope of annual Christmas celebrations at this fine old Victorian-era Tuscan-style house:

> *For Christmas 2008, a twelve-foot tree donated by Michael and Joyce Wilson of Lewisburg greeted guests. It was adorned with fragile 19th century hand-blown glass ornaments and vintage scrap—constructed of highly colorful lithographed decals embellished with tinsel and crepe paper. Small candles were clipped to the edges of branches. During Victorian times, the candles would have been lighted briefly on Christmas Eve or Christmas Day, and there would have been a bucket of water nearby!*

The dining room, with a chandelier in the shape of Victorian gasoliers, is decorated in a typical Victorian fashion, with garlands streaming from the chandelier to the top of the dining table.

The Victorian era celebrated family life, so children and their toys and entertainment were important. "The tree was accented with a number of toys that would have delighted any Victorian child on Christmas morning," Gary notes. Of particular interest, he points out, was a Punch-and-Judy Theatre loaned for the occasion by Douglas and Beatriz Parker of Lewisburg. "It was replete

Vintage ornaments and toys and a hand-crafted creche add to the dominant sense of nostalgia of Slifer House, home to the Slifer family until 1908.

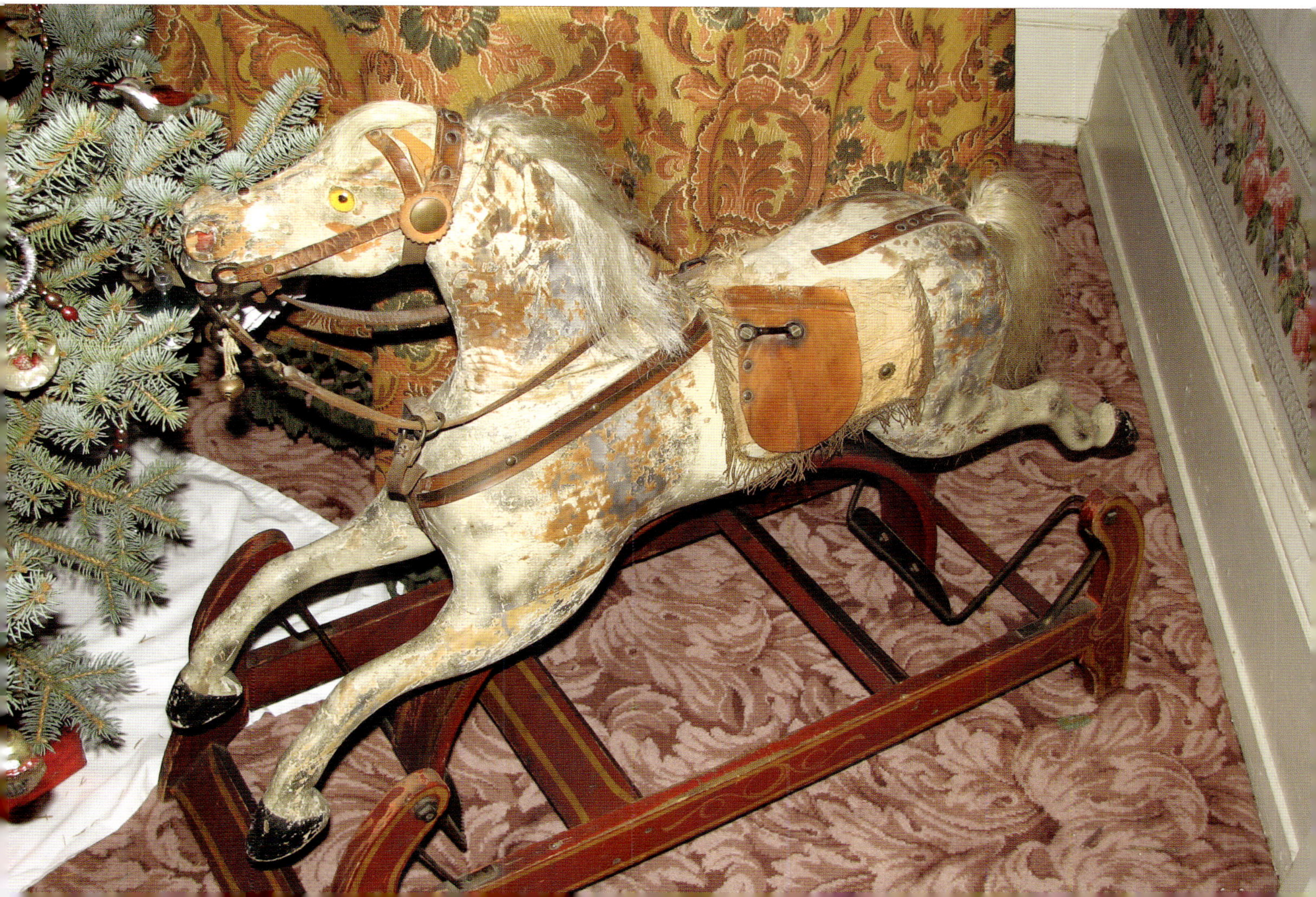

"The tree was accented with a number of toys that would have delighted any Victorian child on Christmas morning,"

Vintage ornaments and toys and a hand-crafted creche add to the dominant sense of nostalgia of Slifer House, home to the Slifer family until 1908.

with puppets representing Punch, the Judge, the Constable, and the ghost," says Gary.

The always elegant Slifer dining room was especially glamorous during the Christmas holidays. "Christmas 2008 decorations included a garland of greenery and white roses suspended from the gas chandelier, creating a tent-like effect over the table. The treatment was based on an 1882 illustration from *Harper's Bazar,*" Gary states.

Creches are universally key Christmas decorations. In 2008, at the Slifer House gallery, there was a special exhibit of creches and nativity scenes in a variety of materials, including wood, ceramic, glass, stained glass, textiles, paper mache, and wax—all from private collections.

According to creche legend, in 1223 in Greccio, Italy, St. Francis wanted observers to experience the Bethlehem setting," says Gary. "So he re-created it by placing an ox, an ass, and some sheep in a manger-like setting, with an infant on a bed of straw. As parishioners came for midnight Mass, they were charmed and deeply moved. Some claimed that when St. Francis lifted the child into his arms, the child wakened and raised his hand in blessing. Through ensuing centuries, craftsmen and artists have fashioned figures out of a wide variety of materials, many adorned with precious metals and jewels. Families displayed them in their homes, attesting to their religious convictions.

Brief history

Slifer House was built during the early days of the Civil War by Eli Slifer, a successful businessman who had started work as an orphan at age 16. When he began building his home. Slifer was in the midst of a second term as Treasurer of the Commonwealth of Pennsylvania. He was asked by the Governor to serve as Secretary of the Commonwealth for

The Christmas tree is decorated as it would have been during the time the Slifers were at home. Over those years, Eli was a member of the Pennsylvania assembly, a state senator, Treasurer of the Commonwealth, and finally Secretary of the Commonwealth during the Civil War.

the duration of the Civil War. "The house, designed by Philadelphia architect Samuel Sloan, was built in an area known as Delta Place. An elegant structure, it was featured in *Godey's Lady's Book*, a popular magazine," says Gary.

The Slifer family lived in the house until Eli's death in 1908, when the house was sold to Dr. Lamont Ross, who sold it to the Evangelical Association in 1916. Changes took place through the years that transformed the property into a skilled care facility, the beginnings of the complex now known as RiverWoods. In July 1976, Slifer House became a museum dedicated to preserving the history of Eli Slifer and his contribution to the area and the state of Pennsylvania Two goals for the House Museum is preservation and education. Education is, of course, an important part of celebrating Christmas as it would have been celebrated in the heyday of Slifer House.

Sherwood-Davidson House

24

Newark, Ohio

Note for the holiday calendar: **Christmas in Veterans' Park!**

"This annual event occurs on the first Saturday of December in Newark, Ohio, when three neighbors—the Sherwood-Davidson House, National Heisey Glass Museum, and Buckingham Meeting House—welcome all to the holiday season," says Emily Larson, Curator of the Sherwood-Davidson House. Emily adds:

For Christmas in Veterans' Park, our sidewalks are illuminated with paper luminaries that lead to the National Heisey Glass Museum on one side, and the Buckingham Meeting House on the other. The Buckingham Meeting House, a ca. 1835 Green Revival style house and gathering place for the Licking County Historical Society, offers refreshments, entertainment, a children's craft, and Santa! The National Heisey Glass Museum also features holiday displays and a children's craft.

1-2 The Sherwood Davidson house is considered one of the finest examples of Federal style architecture in the Ohio Valley. During the Christmas season, the carved fan above the door is fitted with a traditional fruit-and-greenery spray. *Photographs by Bobbi Meldahl, Ryan Meldahl, and Emily Larson, courtesy The Sherwood-Davidson House*

3 Chairs in the foyer were salvaged from the judge's chambers in the third Licking County Courthouse.

At the Sherwood-Davidson House, re-enacters mingle with visitors and provide vignettes, while a string ensemble plays in the parlor. Larson says:

> *There are no records of how either the Sherwoods or Davidsons celebrated Christmas. We do know that the Davidsons were prominent residents of Newark, and were quite well off. Among the fine collections of antique furniture, clocks, china, silver, glass, textiles, toys, and paintings are numerous items in the house that belonged to the Davidsons. We choose to interpret the house as it would have been in their era—during the Civil War. So, there are multiple Christmas trees, sumptuously set tables, nine differently decorated mantles, and beautiful costume displays.*
>
> *The ten-room house underwent a comprehensive four-year 're-restoration' refurbishment (2003-2007) involving flooring, light fixtures, hardware, hand-screened wallpaper, period paint colors, and window coverings. The results will delight all who visit this gracious home.*

In the Victorian-style parlor stands the oldest item in the museum's collection—a case clock made in Amsterdam, Holland ca. 1740, brought to Newark by the Kings, a Quaker family, in the 1830s. The tree is decorated with Christmas cards and crocheted snowflakes.

The tabletop feather tree in Mr. Davidson's library is decorated with old keys from the museum's collection. Whale oil lamps are on the mantel. The bookcase belonged to the Davidson family.

The Sherwood Davidson house is considered one of the finest examples of Federal style architecture in the Ohio Valley.

4

5

4-7 A pier mirror in the dining room reflects a Christmas tree decorated with teacups from the museum's collection. The real-fruit pineapple centerpiece continues a tradition seen in the homes of early colonial settlers along America's eastern seaboard.

7

8

9

10

11

7 In the primitive kitchen—which manages to look quite stylish—cookies are being rolled out on the center table. The tree is decorated with delicious edibles—cookies, nuts, cranberries, and dried apple slices. A collection of pewter ware decorates the mantel.

8 Trees with themes were a big hit. This one—in an upstairs bedroom—is hung with decorative hats. Hat boxes are displayed at tree base.

9-10 The master bedroom features a tree decorated with shoes and boots from the museum's large collection of period clothing. Two Civil War era women's day gowns are displayed. On the Victorian horse-hair covered settee is a tussie-mussie (flower holder) filled with greenery. On a table behind the sofa is an oil lamp.

11 The upstairs sitting room—where Cornelia Davidson entertained close friends and family—is fitted with a Wehrle stove (Wehrle Stove Factory, Newark, Ohio, ca. 1900), a phonograph and a dulcimer. The tree is bedecked with hats and dried hydrangea.

The house is one of the fine example of Federal architecture in the Ohio Valley, according to Emily. Built in another location ca. 1825 by Buckingham Sherwood, a local merchant, it features such beautiful architectural details as a two-story gallery porch and a pedimented fan door. Larason states, "In 1860, Cornelia Davidson purchased the house. The Davidson family lived there until 1946. In 1947, the Licking County Historical Society saved the house from demolition and moved it to Veterans' Park, restored it, and opened the house as a museum in 1952. Visitors now may experience the elegant lifestyle of Licking County during the 1800s—including a wonderful Christmas."

12-13 A child's bedroom, with its rope trundle bed, has its own tree, patriotically decorated with small American flags.

Billings Farm

25

Woodstock, Vermont

Christmas—declared a legal holiday in Vermont in 1850—was not widely celebrated until the latter part of the 19th century. "Even then, on the farm cows had to be milked, ice cut, and wood sawn for the cook stove and fireplaces," says Curator Robert Benz. "Simple, practical gifts, a special meal, and gathering of friends were noteworthy in an otherwise typical day."

Today, Billings Farm (established in 1871, by Frederick Billings, a native Vermonter known for his work in progressive farming and reforestation) is a premier dairy farm famous for Jersey cows, a breed known for the high butterfat and protein content of its milk and imported by Billings. It is also the scene of much merriment during the Christmas season. Holiday programs and activities include the making of historic ornaments. Period-food cooking sessions fill the house with the delightful smell of shortbread and ginger cookies baking in the wood stove. Indoors, there are musical performances. Outdoors, there are horse-drawn sleigh rides and sledding with 18th century jack jumpers (a single runner topped with a short post and a flat board that serves as a seat).

The multipurpose farm house by Boston architect Frederick W. Stickney at the progressive1890 Billings Farm included an office for the farm manager, an apartment for the manager and his family, a creamery, and an ice house. *Photographs courtesy Billings Farm & Museum.*

The stockings were "hung by the chimney with care"—filled with tasty tidbits including candies, nuts, and raisins.

1

2

3

Farm House interiors are authentically dressed for the Holidays, with decorations typical of the late 1800s. Fresh, fragrant greens are draped lavishly and lovingly over mantels, windows, and doorways. Look about for small trees, packed in a jar or butter tub standing on a table top—as they would have been in a late 1800s house. In the early days, ornaments were handmade by family members who would string cranberries, popcorn or dried apples into ropes to encircle the tree (the use of food for these purposes indicating a sense of bounty, unknown to ancestors who endured leaner times). Apples studded with cloves, oranges (exotic and a real treat), silvered or foil-covered chestnuts, painted pine cones and acorns, and handmade paper ornaments were creative expressions and labors of love.

Gifts were often handmade and homemade fancy mittens, satin bows, and stockings. The stockings were "hung by the chimney with care"—filled with tasty tidbits including candies, nuts, and raisins. "Store-bought" gifts were equally practical.

Billings Farm is no ordinary farm house. In 1889, Boston architect Frederick W. Stickney designed what Frederick Billings considered a "model" farm house. It contained a business office for the farm manager, an apartment for the manager and his family, a creamery, and an adjoining ice house. The structure was completed in 1890, and George Aitken, the farm's first professional manager, moved in with his wife and four daughters. They lived there until Mr. Aitken's death in 1910.

During Mr. Aitken's occupancy, the farm grew from 250 to 2,000 acres. Under Mr. Billing's leadership and Mr. Aitken's management, Billings Farm became one of the finest agricultural operations in Vermont. That legacy has been continued through the stewardship of Billings' granddaughter, Mary French Rockefeller and her husband, the late Laurance Spelman Rockefeller, a noted conservationist, philanthropist, and

1 A costumed re-enacter adds typical handmade period ornaments, including strings of popcorn, to the tall Christmas tree in the living room.

2-3 Atop the living room mantel, a treasured gilded mantel clock sets amidst seasonal greenery, pine cones, and colorful ornaments, while below, hang simple cotton stockings.

developer of great destinations on a philosophy of active partnership between government, the non-profit sector, and business. Great destinations (as part of growing eco-tourism) developed by Mr. Rockefeller include lodges in Grand Tetons, Mauna Kea in Hawaii, Caneel Bay in the Virgin Islands, Dorado Beach I Puerto Rico, and the Woodstock Inn & Resort. In a real sense, Billings Farm is also a great Woodstock, Vermont destination.

Meticulous restoration on the Farm House, a key feature of this working farm (a premiere dairy farm) that is also an active educational institution, began in 1987. A collaborative effort of tradesmen, conservators, curators and researchers, the project involved building analysis and examination of historical material. Scientific paint analysis revealed the original paint colors of the house and receipts confirmed the specific colors chosen.

The result of careful restoration efforts is an authentic Victorian-era building that is a unique multi-faceted farm house. It, and surrounding buildings and grounds provide extraordinary educational opportunities to examine and experience daily elements of Vermont farm life in the 1890s—the mission of this splendid farm.

4 Ropes, fashioned by hand from home-grown evergreen branches, perfume hall stairs, adding welcome color and texture to the somewhat severe interior.

5 *The Billings Farm and Museum Holiday Recipes and Decorations* booklet contains favorite farmhouse recipes for Plum Pudding and other desserts featured on the holiday dining table.

Marjorie Kinnan Rawlings House

26

Cross Creek, Florida

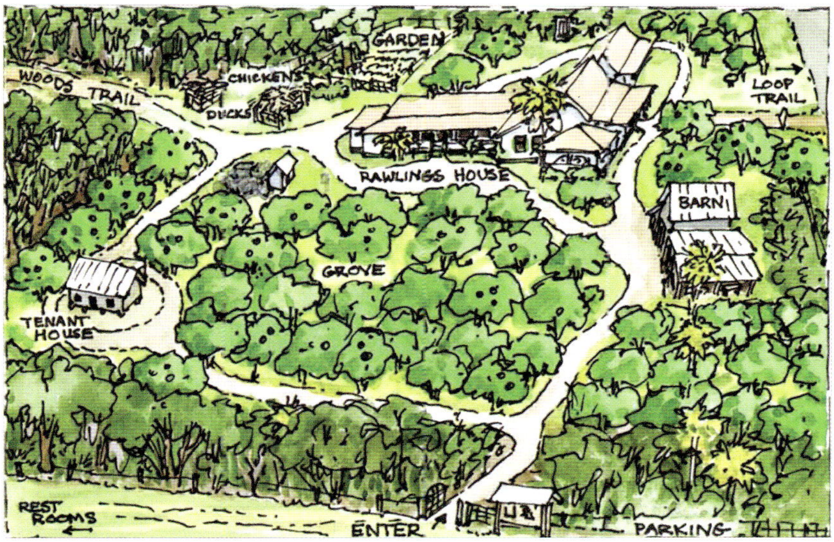

A map of the grounds of Marjorie Kinnan Rawlings' Cross Creek farm in Florida. *Maps courtesy Florida State Parks; photographs by Kathleen Carr, courtesy Florida State Parks*

Christmas in Florida is about much more than just beaches, orange groves and the Everglades. It's about both light and enlightenment—the magic of everyday as it can be experienced at Marjorie Kinnan Rawlings' farm which she called her "place of enchantment."

Christmas at her Cross Creek home today looks very much like the 1930s holidays celebrated by famous authoress Marjorie Kinnan Rawlings. Time seems to stand still in the unpretentious Cracker style farm house, her home for twenty-five years in what was an isolated area of Old Florida.

Rooms, much as she left them, seem to anticipate her momentary return.

In the living room, comfortable overstuffed furniture faces a fireplace with a smoke-covered front that tells of many gatherings around glowing fires. The mantel is simply and beautifully decorated with a single beautiful bowl surrounded by home-grown fruit and found objects from the farm grounds.

In the kitchen, staff members who care for the house and surrounding farm may be cooking! The dishes they are preparing are from recipes found

Kitchen & Pantries
Outhouse
Marjorie Rawlings' Bedroom
Dining Room
South Porch
Guest Bedroom
Guest Bath
Staff Office
Living Room
Front Porch

1

2

Marjorie Kinnan Rawlings House

in Mrs. Rawlings' book *Cross Creek Cookery*. The December 2004 menu for the annual Holiday Party dinner for a supporting group—The Friends of Marjorie Kinnan Rawlings Farm, and their special guests—featured pork pilau, greens, and "all the trimmings."

On the screened front porch—the spot where she did most of her writing—is a round table which was a gift to Marjorie from her husband, Charles, who may have made it. Marjorie's typewriter stands at the ready. It's not difficult to imagine Marjorie sitting there, typing away on the manuscript of *The Yearling*, her story abut a young boy who is forced to decide the fate of a fawn he has raised as a pet.

Marjorie Kinnan Rawlings, a native of Washington, D. C., knew as a young girl that she wanted to be a writer. After graduating from the University of Wisconsin, she married fellow writer Charles Rawlings, and worked as a journalist. They moved to Cross Creek in 1928. She loved the land, its creatures, and her neighbors. Inspired, she began writing short stories. In 1933, she

1-2 Rawlings called her sprawling unpretentious home at Cross Creek her "place of enchantment."

3 A large gaily decorated evergreen Christmas tree adds holiday cheer to a window-walled sitting room. Friends and supporters of Cross Creek gather here annually at Christmas time.

3

It's about both light and enlightenment—the magic of everyday as it can be experienced at Marjorie Kinnan Rawlings' farm which she called her "place of enchantment."

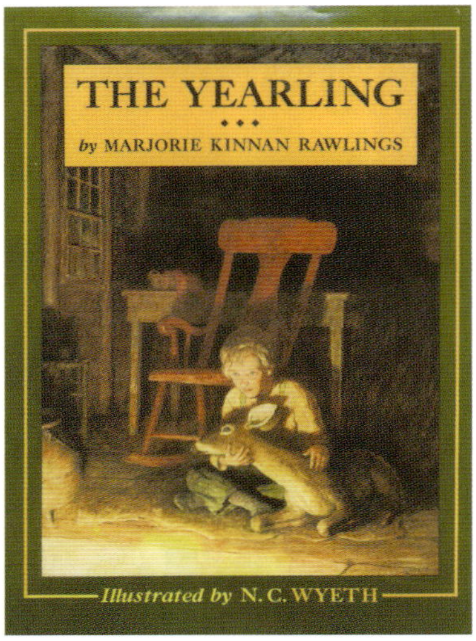

published her first novel, *South Moon Under*, to critical acclaim. It was followed by *The Yearling*, copyrighted in 1938. Illustrations were by famed artist N.C. Wyeth. The book earned Mrs. Rawlings the Pulitzer Prize for fiction in 1939. This touching story of a young boy's devotion to a rescued deer which threatened vital farm crops became a memorable motion picture starring Gregory Peck. Two other works—*Gal Young Un'* and *Cross Creek*, described as an evocative, lyrical love story to a place and a humorous look at her neighbors—also became motion pictures.

Marjorie Kinnan Rawlings' "regional" writings reveal a wider vision of the world—a sense of the cosmic forces that rule the lives of men and women. Her achievements have earned her humble house and farm a "National Historic Landmark"—a designation that acknowledges that significant

Marjorie Kinnan Rawlings, famed for *The Yearling (cover of Scribner Illustrated Classic book, illustrated by N. C. Wyeth)* and other heartwarming tales set in her own rural Florida surroundings, wrote on this screened porch.

historic events occurred in that place, events that expressed the ideas that shaped the nation.

Christmas in Florida is about much more than just beaches, orange groves and the Everglades. It's about Marjorie Kinnan Rawlings' and her insight into the human heart.

4 Home grown fruit piled simply into a porcelain bowl charmingly decorates the living room mantel at Cross Creek farm.

5 A lace tablecloth was a touch of luxury and elegance in the dining room where Rawlings, a noted cook, entertained.

Van Cortlandt Manor

27

Croton-on-Hudson, New York

Van Cortlandt Manor's 300-year history makes it the perfect site for celebrating Christmas as it was enjoyed by well-to-do farm families in America's earliest days.

A white painted, double gate hung with decorative wreathes welcomes visitors. Inside the ancient stone farmhouse, a traditional kissing bell hangs in the hallway. In the parlor, with its Chippendale style sofa, hangs the John Wesley Jarvis portrait of Pierre Van Cortlandt (1721-1814). The dining room table is set for a festive meal. In the large and well-equipped Federal-style kitchen, costumed cooks create meals prepared from foods that might have grown at the Manor a century ago.

In September 1997, this working farm and seat of rural industry celebrated its 300th year, marking the signing of a Royal Patent in 1697 by William III that publicly recognized the Van Cortlandt family's political support to the English monarchy.

The Royal Patent designated the Lordship of Stephanus Van Cortlandt, first and only Lord of Van Cortlandt Manor. Following his Dutch ancestor's custom, Stephanus willed his estate to all his immediate heirs (rather than to the oldest son, as was the English custom).

In 1697, the Manor consisted of 86,000 acres of land near the confluence of the Hudson and Croton Rivers, purchased by Stephanus from native Indian and European owners.

At the time, Stephanus and his wife, Gertruyd Schuyler Van Cortlandt, made the New York (city) house inherited from Stephanus's father Oloff, their home. Oloff had arrived in New Amsterdam as an employee of the Dutch West India company, and stayed to become a wealthy brewer. Stephanus continued that business and began buying land in what is now Westchester County, New York.

1 Christmas wreaths on the gates welcome guests to the 300-year-old Van Cortlandt Manor home of Lord Van Cortlandt, the first and only Lord of the Manor. *Photographs courtesy Historic Hudson Valley/www.hudsonvalley.org*

2 Costumed guides hang the traditional kissing ball in the hallway.

Inside the ancient stone house farmhouse, a traditional kissing bell hangs in the hallway.

Stephanus's son, Philip, inherited the property in 1732. At Philip's death, one son, Stephen inherited the house in New York City; another, Pierre, moved with his wife and infant son Philip to the 1,225-acre Manor. The enterprising Pierre made the manor a self-sufficient enterprise and added 3,138 acres in one 1758 transaction. A shrewd businessman, Pierre added sawmill, gristmills, and a ferry service. His land leasing practices were innovative and his farming interests commercial rather than mere subsistence farming.

The family history is the stuff of novels, yet it is very real and an authentic part of America's growth from virgin woodland to sophisticated society. Over the years, nine generations of Van Cortlandts owned Van Cortlandt Manor. In 1945, it was sold to a man named Otis Taylor. After Taylor's death, the man who bought the manor tore down the barns and built a drive-in theater!

Wearing period dress, young people pose as guests enjoying traditional holiday refreshments in the dining room.

Van Cortlandt Manor

In 1953, John D. Rockefeller, Jr. bought the manor house and began to do what the Rockefeller family does so well—restore yet another significant piece of American history. Today, Van Cortlandt Manor—a jewel of the beautiful Hudson River Valley—is one of several sites comprising Historic Hudson Valley museums. (Other sites include: Washington Irving's Sunnyside, Philipsburg Manor and Kykuit (the Rockefeller Estate), Union Church of Pocantico Hills, and Montgomery Place Historic Estate).

Once again, the Van Cortlandt Manor is a hub of much activity, a bustling enterprise, and the scene of exciting events throughout the year. To visit this venerable manor (only an hour's drive north of New York City) on weekdays during the Christmas season is to see the holiday through the eyes of earlier generations and to witness domestic life as it was lived by a patriot family just after the American Revolution.

3 The parlor, with its handsomly carved mantel and painted corner cabinet, features a portrait of founder Stephanus Van Cortlandt's son, Pierre (1721-1814) who greatly expanded the Manor and its businesses.

4 The Van Cortlandt's kitchen—one of the largest, best-equipped Federal-period kitchens in America—features open-hearth cooking. During the holidays, a costumed cook demonstrates.

Campbell House

28

Spokane, Washington

The Campbell House in Spokane is a splendid example of the Tudor Revival style. To visit the mansion is to glimpse life in Spokane as it was lived during the Age of Elegance. There are fabulous decorations, historic-foods cooking demonstrations, carols around the piano, and storytelling. There is also the 2003 National Council on Public History award-winning tour that takes the form of a participatory historical novel. Visitors become period characters—a maid, politician, detective—people associated with the Campbell family. All in good fun,

This splendid house was built by a well-to-do mining investor. Fortunes were waiting to be made in the 1880s, when Amasa Campbell and John A. Finch were sent by Youngstown, Ohio investors to investigate more closely Idaho's famed Coeur d'Alene Mining District. Quick to see the possibilities Campbell and Finch became partners, invested in mines and soon were earning thousands of dollars a month.

Campbell went back to Ohio to marry Grace Fox, a schoolteacher.

At first, the couple lived in Idaho, where their daughter, Helen, was born in 1892. In 1898, Mr. Campbell moved his family away from Idaho's booming but troubled mining district to Spokane, Washington. Spokane was safer and offered more social and schooling opportunities for Helen.

With guests or alone, the Campbells dined in the formal dining room, situated four steps above the entry floor. At Christmastime, the ceiling was draped tent-like with evergreen garlands. *Photograph by Dean Davis, courtesy Northwest Museum of Arts & Culture, Spokane, Washington*

1

2

To build their home the Campbells called on renowned Spokane architect Kirtland K. Cutter, who designed a Tudor Revival style mansion with its characteristic brick, stucco, sandstone, and heavy half-timber exterior. The house was built in 1898, on a prominent bluff in a neighborhood known as Browne's Addition. From the deep verandah at the rear of the house, there is a commanding view of the Spokane River gorge. The home includes an offset service wing and an adjacent carriage house. The Campbell's considerable household staff (two maids, cook, coachman, and gardener) lived onsite. Women servants had rooms on the third floor of the main house, while the male servants resided above the carriage house.

The Campbells, assisted by an interior decorator, furnished the home with such fineries as Persian carpets, velvet draperies, new furniture,

1 In the darkly paneled entry hall, large-scaled floral wallpaper reminiscent of the William Morris style, forms a colorful backdrop for the heavily carved newel post with its decorative light fixture. On the left side of the hall is the library; on the right in dramatic contrast is the light, bright French reception room. *Photograph by Dean Davis; All photographs courtesy Northwest Museum of Arts & Culture, Spokane, Washington*

2 A shaped ceiling and handsome exposed wood beams lend an elegant hunting lodge look to the Library of the English Tudor Revival style Campbell House by Spokane architect Kirtland K. Cutter. *Photograph by Dean Davis*

3

4

3-4 In the spacious family room, the tree becomes the focal point at Christmas time. The Campbell's daughter, Helen learned to play on an upright piano like the one in the corner. *Photograph by Dean Davis*

and a basement-level gambling room where Mr. Campbell and his friends might retreat to play cards and enjoy cigars. The library, with its looming sandstone fireplace with cozy inglenooks, provided space for reading, quiet conversation, board games and music. The Campbells also relied on this spacious room for dances, weddings, and funerals. The French rococo reception room, all pink silk and gilding, gave Mrs. Campbell a place to receive social callers, an important ritual of late Victorian life. The house also included some of the latest technologies: a central heating system with concealed radiators, electric lighting, a servant call box, and a telephone.

Mr. Campbell died in 1912. When Mrs. Campbell died in 1924, Helen gave Campbell House to the Eastern Washington State Historical Society, which made it a museum. Once a new museum building was opened in 1960, restoration work was begun to return Campbell House to its Age of Elegance glory. Curator Patti Larkin says, "The beauty of Campbell House is that it is more than a wonderfully restored grand home. We know about the family and servants who lived and worked there, and about the community that surrounded them. The house brings Spokane's early 20th century history to life for its visitors."

"The beauty of Campbell House is that it is more than a wonderfully restored grand home."

5

5 An early photograph of the Campbell house, with an early model automobile parked curbside. At the back of the house, a deep veranda affords a view of the Spokane River below.

6 A doll and stuffed bear in a chair near the living room Christmas tree are reminders that Amasa Campbell, who made a fortune in mining, wrote of decorating the tree for his daughter, Helen. *Photograph by Dean Davis*

7 Grace Campbell entertained callers in her French Revival-style reception room with its extravagantly decorative gilded mantel. *Photograph by Dean Davis*

6

7

Deck The Halls

29

Tips at Vaile and Bingham-Waggoner, Independence, Missouri

Each Christmas in Independence, Missouri, the elegant Vaile Mansion and grand Bingham-Waggoner Estate become designer showcase houses, chock full of exciting holiday decorating ideas. The area's top designers who create the glorious fantasies are happy to share their ideas. Here are tips from the gifted Santa's helpers at Vaile and Bingham-Waggoner.

Wake Up Bedrooms

HIGHLIGHT AN ARCHITECTURAL FEATURE *(bow or bay window, or a niche) with a lighted evergreen swag that transforms the area into a stunning focal point.* Shelia Gilliam, Krystal Perkinds, Belinda Mayfield, Hollie Markley-Schmuhl, Decorators

ADD DRAMA TO THE BEDROOM *by flanking the bed with matching trees embellished with ornaments in colors inspired by the room's color scheme.* Allie Markley, Shelia Gilliam, Krystal Perkinds, Belinda Mayfield, Hollie Markley-Schmuhl, Decorators

ALTER PROPORTIONS VISUALLY. *Add height to too-low furnishings by placing decorations above—like an elegant garland and a wreath adorned with a trumpet.* Allie Markley, Shelia Gilliam, Krystal Perkinds, Belinda Mayfield, Hollie Markley-Schmuhl, Decorators

All photographs in this chapter are by Janeen Aggen, courtesy Independence, Missouri, Tourism.

Dress Chair Backs for Dinner

DECORATE DINING ROOM CHAIR BACKS. *Give plain-Jane chairs holiday pizzazz by tying large ribbon bows with streamers to the backsides of slatted chairs.* Inspired by Shawn Sullivan, Decorator

MAKE A RIBBON WREATH. *Cover a plastic wreath form with bows (use glue gun or stickpins), or wind ribbon around a plastic wreath and highlight with a large bow.* Inspired by Shawn Sullivan, Decorator

Kitchens In Good Taste

SET THE SCENE FOR SANTA'S ARRIVAL *with a plate of colorful Christmas cookies, a decorative cup, and a pot that could be full of hot chocolate near the fireplace. In the kitchen, pile gingerbread cookies on a large wooden tray! Add a wooden rolling pin.* Pam Slade, Designer

TUCK A GINGERBREAD HOUSE *(or several) inside an open cabinet or show off a group on the countertop, surround with greenery, and light up the arrangement with tiny white fairy lights.* Shawn Sullivan and Nancy Ward, Decorators

Make Mantels Magical

PLAY UP PINK *as a pretty option for red. Decorate with pink ornaments and ribbon accented with glittering metallic golds and silvers.* Carolyn Haynes, Decorator

EMPHASIZE A THEME THAT SUGGESTS DECORATIONS. *A Music Room should have music as the theme. Emphasize it by incorporating musical instruments like beautiful old violins into tabletop displays, hanging toy horns on the tree, displaying a beautiful harp, using old sheet music in displays and vignettes.* Pam Slade, Designer

CHOOSE A COLOR PALETTE THAT SUITS THE ROOM. *The theme "Victorian Silver," chosen for 2010 Christmas, called for lots of silver decorations and adding "accent" colors of gold, copper, and Tiffany blue to match the décor of the room.* Pam Slade, Designer

Give Stairs Star Treatment

BE DRAMATIC—*pair a stai- and tree. Use silver tissue lame as garland for a Christmas tree near the stair. Swag the fabric from the top of the stair railing to the top of the tree, letting it curl around the tree to the floor.* Yvonne Evans, Diane Evans, Tori Michael, Marilyn Jones, Decorators

Turn Tabletops Into Visual Feasts

USE AVAILABLE ITEMS TO SAVE TIME AND MONEY. *A crystal or glass compote filled with ornaments is an easy, elegant mantel decoration. On the coffee table, set a silver coffee service enlivened with a sprig of greenery and holly berries.* Pam Slade, Designer

Fun With Toys

DECORATE WITH TOYS. *Add children's toys and trinkets to displays on cabinets (old stoves, too), tabletops, and around the base of the tree.* Joann Howell, Scott Howell, Jay Turner, Decorators

MIX FAUX AND REAL. *Give a faux snowman a real fresh carrot nose. Be prepared to refresh the decoration frequently!* Pat Launius and Karen Plourde, Decorators

Oh! Tannenbaums

ADD DIMENSION TO THE CHRISTMAS TREE *by decorating inside/out. Start by placing solid-colored or gently worn ornaments deep in the branches and work your way outward. Finish by placing the prettiest, most ornate ornaments on the outside.* Carolyn Haynes, Designer

GIVE THE TREE AN ETHEREAL INNER GLOW. *Light the tree from the inside out, so that it looks as though the tree were glowing all over. Add lights before hanging ornaments.* Pam Slade, Decorator

FILL UP BARE SPOTS IN THE TREE *with faux flowers, large ornaments, toys, tree top angels, toy Santas, or any suitable item in a size and scale to suit the tree.* Pam Slade, Decorator

HIGHLIGHT A SPECIAL ORNAMENT *by putting a snowflake or a small mirror ornament behind it.* Pam Slade, Decorator

ADD AN UNUSUAL DECORATION. *An upside-down Christmas tree—especially a flocked one—is attention-getting and sets a room apart.* Pam Slade, Designer

BE COLORFULLY CONVENTIONAL. *Decorate the Christmas tree with old-fashioned red (or pink) ribbons, red ornaments, and red-and-white striped candy canes.* Nancy Ward and Shawn Sullivan, Decorators

DECORATE THE CHRISTMAS TREE WITH RIBBON BOWS. *Forget the ornaments and just use bows—large or small, depending on the size of your tree. Hang bows lavishly on Christmas tree boughs. Choose a solid color or traditional plaid pattern.* Inspired by Shawn Sullivan, Decorator

ADD IMPACT TO ORNAMENTS WITH RIBBON TIES. *Tie ornaments onto the tree branches with narrow ribbon bows. Give bows long streamers for tall trees, short streamers (tails) for small trees.* Inspired by Shawn Sullivan, Decorator

MATCH RIBBON AND ORNAMENT COLORS *for monotone color schemes for trees. (For multi-color schemes, contrast ribbon and ornament colors.)* Inspired by Shawn Sullivan, Decorator

ADD HOLIDAY DECORATIONS TO "EVERYDAY" ACCESSORIES. *Instead of putting away un-seasonal accessories, surround them with Christmas greenery. For example, tuck a sprig of holly around a favorite photograph. Surround candlesticks with evergreen boughs wreath-like and accent with festive ribbon.* Carolyn Haynes, Designer

ADD GLAMOUR TO FAUX FLOWERS—*spray them with glitter or diamond dust for greater elegance.* Pam Slade, Decorator

USE PINE CONES AS ORNAMENTS—*they look great on a tree and the price is right, natural or painted.* Pam Slade, Decorator

CREATE AN "ANTIQUE" TREE ORNAMENT. *Wrap a Styrofoam ball in an antique hankie, gather with a ribbon tie and hang on a tree with an antique theme.* Pam Slade, Decorator

GARLAND KEY FURNISHINGS—*call attention to a mirror that multiplies the impact of an elegant design.* Sheila Gilliam, Krystal Perkinds, Belinda Mayfield, Hollie Markley-Schmuhl, Decorators

Wreaths Welcome

USE WREATHS HERE, THERE, AND EVERYWHERE.

Directory of Historic House Museums

Contact Information

Historic House museums welcome all year 'round, but are at their most glorious during the Christmas Season. Here is contact information for the Historic Houses featured in the authors' books *Christmas At Historic Houses*, *Decorating for Christmas at Historic Houses*, and *Delicious Christmas Decorations at Historic Houses*.

Adams House
22 Van Buren Street
Deadwood, South Dakota 57732
Tel: 605.578.3724
www. adamsmusuemandhouse.org

Baldwin-Reynolds House
(PO Box 411)
639 Terrace Street
Meadville, PA 16335
Tel: 814.671.1030
e.m jsherretts@baldwinreynolds.org

Bartow-Pell Mansion Museum
895 Shore Road, Pelham Bay Park
The Bronx, New York 10464
Tel: 718.885.1461
info@bpmm.org

Bidwell House Museum
100 Art School Road
PO Box 537
Monterey, MA 01245
Tel: 413.528.6888
e.m bidwellhouse@gmail.com

Billings Farm and Museum
5302 River Road, P.O. Box 489
Woodstock, Vermont 0509
Tel: 802.457.2335
www.billingsfarm.org

Biltmore Estate
1 Approach Road
Asheville, North Carolina 28803
Tel: 800.624.1575 or 828-225-1333
www.biltmore.com

Bingham-Waggoner Home and Estate
313 West Pacific
Independence, Missouri 64050
Tel: 816.461.3491
Fax: 816.461.1540
www.bwestate.org

Blithewold Mansion, Gardens and Arboretum
101 Ferry Road
Bristol, Rhode Island 02809
Tel: 401.253.2707
www.blithewold.org

Butterworth Center
1105-8th Street
Moline, Illinois 61265
Tel: 309.765.7970
www.butterworthcenter.com

Calvin B. Taylor House Museum
PO Box 351
208 North Main St.
Berlin, MD 21811
TaylorHouseMuseum@Verizon.net

Campbell House Museum
1508 Locust St.
St. Louis, MO 63103
Tel: 314.421.0325
e.m campbellhm@earthlink.net

Campbell House
2316 W. First Avenue
Spokane, WA 99204
Tel: 509.456.3931
themac@northwestmuseum.org

Charleston Museum
(Joseph Manigault House)
360 Meeting St.
Charleston, SC 29403
Tel: 843.722.2996, x 235
www.charlestonmuseum.or

Chief Vann House Historic Site
82 Georgia Highway 225 N
Chatsworth, Georgia 30705
Tel: 706.695.2598
www.gastateparks.org/info/chiefvann/

Directory of Historic House Museums

Chinqua Penn Plantation
2138 Wentworth
Reidsville, NC 27320
Tel: 336.349.4576
e.m lisa@chinquapenn.com

Colonial Williamsburg Foundation
P. O. Box 1776
Williamsburg, VA 23187-1776
Tel: 757.229.1000
www.history.org/history

Crocker House Museum
15 Union Street
Mount Clemens, MI 48043
Tel: 586.465.2488,
Fax: 586.465.2932
e.m crockerhousemuseum@sbcglobal.net

David Davis Mansion
1000 E. Monroe Drive
Bloomington, Illinois 61701
Tel: 309.828,1084
Fax: 309.828.3493
e.m davismansion@yahoo.com

Deere-Wiman House
817-11th Avenue
Moline, Illinois 61265
Tel: 309.765.7970
www.butterworthcenter.com

Drayton Hall
3380 Ashley River Road
Charleston, South Carolina 29414
Phone: 843.769.2600
www.draytonhall org

Egypt Plantation Museum
(Heard-Northington House)
PO Box 219
Egypt, TX 77436-0219
egypt@wcnet.net
www.egypttexas.org

Emlen Physick Estate
1048 Washington Street
Cape May, New Jersey 08204
Tel: 800.275.4278 or 609.884-5404
Fax: 609.884.2006
e.m mac4arts@capemaymac.org
www.capemaymac.org

Florence Griswold Museum
96 Lyme Street
Old Lyme, Connecticut 06371
Tel: 860.434.5542
www.flogris.org

Gallier House
(Hermann-Grima & Gallier Houses)
20 Saint Louis Street
New Orleans, LA 70112
Tel: 504.525.5661
e.m HGrimaGallier@aol.com
www.hgghh.org

Hazelwood Historic House Museum
1008 South Monroe Avenue
Greenbay, Wisconsin 54305
Tel: 920.437.1840
e.m bchs@netnet.net
www.browncohistoricalsoc.org/hazelwood

Hearthside Homestead
677 Great Road
Lincoln, RI 02865
Tel: 401.726.0597
e.m kathy.hartley@hearthsidehouse.org

Hearthstone Historic House Museum
625 W. Prospect
Appleton, Wisconsin 54911
Tel: 920.730.8204
www.focol.org/hearthstone

Hermann-Grima & Gallier Houses
20 Saint Louis Street
New Orleans, LA 70112
Tel: 504.525.5661
e.m HGrimaGallier@aol.com
www.hgghh.org

Joel Lane Museum House
PO Box 10884
Raleigh, NC 27605 (US mail)
728 W. Hargett St.
Raleigh, NC 27603
Tel 919.833.3431
Fax: 919.833.9431
e.m joellane@bellsouth.net

John Lind Home
622 Center Street
New Ulm, Minnesota 56073
Tel: 507.354.8802
e.m lindhouse@newulmtel.net
www.lindhouse.org

Joseph Manigault House
350 Meeting Street
Charleston, South Carolina
Phone: 843.722.2996
e.m info@charlestonmuseum.org
www.charlestonmuseum.org

Lyndon Baines Johnson Ranch
P.O. Box 329
Johnson City, TX 78636
Tel: 830.868.7128
www.nps.gov/lyjo/

Leu House Museum
1920 N. Forest Avenue
Orlando, FL 32803-1537
Tel: 407.246.2620
Fax 407.246.2849
e.m rbowden@cityoforlando.net
www.leugardens.org

Jail, Marshal's Home and Museum
217 North Main Street
Independence, Missouri 64050
Tel: 816.252.1892
www.jchs.org.

Marjorie Kinnan Rawlings Farm
18700 South CR 325
Cross Creek, Florida 32640
Tel: 352.466.3672
www.marojiekinnanrawlings.org

Maymont Mansion
1700 Hampton St.
Richmond, VA 23220
Tel: 804.358.7166, x 329
e.m info@maymont.org
www.maymont.org

Molly Brown House Museum
1340 Pennsylvania Street
Denver, Colorado 80203
Tel: 303.832.4092
Tel: 303.832.2340
www.mollybrown.org

Monticello
P.O. Box 316
Charlottesville, Virginia 22902
Tel: 434.984.9822
www.monticello.org

Morris Butler House
1204 North Park Avenue
Indianapolis, Indiana 46202
Tel: 317.636.5409
Fax: 317.636.2630
e.m mbhouse@historiclandmarks.org
www.historiclandmarks.org

Mount Clare
Carroll Park
1500 Washington Blvd
Baltimore, Maryland 21230
Tel: 410.837.3262
www.montclare.org

Mount Vernon
Mount Vernon Ladies' Association
PO Box 110
Mount Vernon, VA 22121
Tel: 703.780.2000
www.mountvernon.org

My Old Kentucky Home
(Federal Hill)
501 East Stephen Foster Avenue
Bardstown, Kentucky 40004-0323
Tel: 502.348.3502
MyOldKentuckyHome@ky.gov
www.parks.ky.gov/stateparks/mk/

Oldfields–Lilly House and Gardens
4000 Michigan Road
Indianapolis, Indiana 46208-3325
Tel: 317.923.1331
www.ima-art.org

Petersen House Museum
1414 W. Southern Avenue
Tempe, AZ 85282
www.museum@tempe.gov

Pettengill-Morron House
1212 W. Moss Avenue
Peoria, IL 61606
Tel: 309.674.1921
Fax 309.674.1882
www.peoriahistoricalsociety.org

Physick House
(Emlen Physick Estate)
1048 Washington Street
Cape May, New Jersey 08204
Tel:: 800.275.4278 or 609.884-5404
Fax: 609.884.2006
e.m mac4arts@capemaymac.org
www.capemaymac.org

Pittock Mansion
3229 NW Pittock Drive
Portland, Oregon 97210
Tel: 503.823.3624
www.pittockmansion.com

Richards-DAR House Museum
256 North Joachim Street
Mobile, AL 36603
Tel: 251.208.7320
2638smbg@bellsouth.net
www.richardsdarhouse.com

Riversdale House Museum
4811 Riversdale Road
Riverdale Park, MD 20737
Tel: 301.864.0420
e.m ann.wass@pgparks.com
www.pgparks.com

Roseland Cottage (Bowen House)
556 Rte. 169,
Woodstock, CT
www.historicewengland.org

Samuel Cupples House at St. Louis University
3673 West Pine Mall
St. Louis, MO 63108
Tel 314.977.3575
Fax 314.977.3581
www.cupples slu.edu

The Sherwood-Davidson House Museum
Veterans' Park
PO Box 785
Newark, OH 43058-0785
Tel: 740.345.4898
e.m sherwooddavidson@yahoo.co
www.lchs@alink.com

Slifer House Museum
80 Magnolia Drive
Lewisburg, PA 17837
Tel: 570.524.2245
e.m Gary.parks@albrightcare.org
www.albrightcare.org/slifer-house

Tudor Place Historic House and Garden
1644 31st Street NW
Washington, DC 20007
Tel: 202.965.0400
Fax: 202.965.0164
e.m info@tudorplace.org
www.tudorplace.org

Vaile Mansion - De Witt Museum
1500 North Liberty
Independence, Missouri 64050
Tel: 816 325-7430
www.vailemansion.org

Van Cortlandt Manor
525 South Riverside Avenue
Croton-on-Hudson, NY 10520
Tel: 914.271.8981
e.m info@hudsonvalley.org
www.hudsonvalley.org

Villa Finale
401 King William Street
San Antonio, Texas 78204

Villa Finale Visitor Center
122 Madison Street
San Antonio, Texas 78204
Tel: 210-223-9800
www.VillaFinale.org

Waddesdon Manor
Nr Aylesbury
Buckinghamshire
HP18 OJH
United Kingdom
Tel: +44(0) 1296 658586
Fax: +44(0) 1296 653212
e.m waddesdonmanor@nationaltrust.org.uk
www.waddesdon.org.uk

Wade House
W7824 Center Street
PO Box 34
Greenbush, WI 33026
Tel 920.526.3271
Fax? 920.526.3626
David.simmons@wisconsinhistory.org
www.wadehouse.org

Webb-Deane-Stevens Museum
211 Main St.
Wethersfield, CT 06109
Tel: 860-529-0612, x14
e.m clyle@webb-deane-stevens.org
www.webb-deane-stevens.org

White House
1600 Pennsylvania Avenue
Washington, D.C. 20500
Tel: 202.456.7041

White House Visitor Center
Southeast corner of 15th and E Streets
Washington, DC 20500
www.whitehouse.gov

Whitehall, Henry Morrison Flagler Museum
One Whitehall Way
P.O. Box 969
Palm Beach, Florida 33480
Tel: 561.655.2833
www.flaglermuseum.us